Student Guide with Map Exercises

THE ENDURING VISION

A HISTORY OF THE AMERICAN PEOPLE

CONCISE FOURTH EDITION

Volume 1: To 1877

Paul S. Boyer • Clifford E. Clark, Jr.
Sandra McNair Hawley
Joseph F. Kett • Neal Salisbury • Harvard Sitkoff
Nancy Woloch

Barbara Blumberg
Pace University

HOUGHTON MIFFLIN COMPANY   BOSTON   NEW YORK

Sponsoring Editor: Colleen Shanley Kyle
Editorial Associate: Michael Kerns
Editorial Assistant: Tamara Bhalla
Manufacturing Coordinator: Florence Cadran
Senior Marketing Manager: Sandra McGuire

Copyright © 2002 by Houghton Mifflin Company. All rights reserved.

No part of this work may be reproduced or transmitted in any form or by any means, electronic or mechanical, including photocopying and recording, or by any information storage or retrieval system without the prior written permission of Houghton Mifflin Company unless such copying is expressly permitted by federal copyright law. Address inquiries to College Permissions, Houghton Mifflin Company, 222 Berkeley Street, Boston, MA 02116-3764.

Printed in the U.S.A.

ISBN: 0-618-10202-7

123456789-CRS-02 01 00 99 98

Contents

Preface   v

Chapter 1   America Begins   1

Chapter 2   Transatlantic Encounters and Colonial Beginnings, 1492–1630   9

Chapter 3   Expansion and Diversity: The Rise of Colonial America   24

Chapter 4   Colonial Society Comes of Age, 1660–1750   39

Chapter 5   The Road to Revolution, 1744–1776   51

Chapter 6   The Forge of Nationhood, 1776–1788   64

Chapter 7   Launching the New Republic, 1789–1800   77

Chapter 8   Jeffersonianism and the Era of Good Feelings   89

Chapter 9   The Transformation of American Society, 1815–1840   100

Chapter 10   Politics, Religion, and Reform in Antebellum America   109

Chapter 11   Life, Leisure, and Culture, 1840–1860   119

Chapter 12   The Old South and Slavery, 1800–1860   128

Chapter 13   Immigration, Expansion, and Sectional Conflict, 1840–1848   136

Chapter 14   From Compromise to Secession, 1850–1861   147

Chapter 15   Reforging the Union: Civil War, 1861–1865   158

Chapter 16   The Crises of Reconstruction, 1865–1877   170

Preface

This *Student Guide with Map Exercises* is intended to help you to master the history presented in *The Enduring Vision: A History of the American People,* Concise Fourth Edition. It is not a substitute for reading the textbook. However, used properly as a supplement to the textbook, it should assist you in focusing on the important events, issues, and concepts in U.S. history, as well as on the people whose ideas and actions help us to understand the past. It is also designed to build your vocabulary and to improve your knowledge of geography.

Each chapter in the *Student Guide* corresponds to a chapter in *The Enduring Vision,* Concise Fourth Edition, and is divided into the following sections:

- **Outline.** This handy reference and study tool follows the outline of the textbook chapter. You should skim it before reading the textbook chapter to get an overview of the contents. Then carefully read the textbook chapter itself. After completing the textbook chapter, reread the outline as a review.

- **Vocabulary.** This section defines social-science terms and other words used in the textbook chapter that may be new to you. Look over the list before you read the textbook chapter. Familiarize yourself with any words that you do not already know.

- **Identifications.** Here you will find the important persons, laws, terms, groups, and events covered in *The Enduring Vision,* Concise Third Edition. After reading the textbook chapter, test yourself by identifying who or what each item was and how this person or thing fits into the overall story. That is, what is its historical significance?

- **Skill Building: Maps.** In many chapters of the *Student Guide,* you will find map exercises asking you to locate places mentioned in the text chapter and to explain the historical significance of those places.

- **Multiple-Choice Questions, Essay Questions, and Answers to Multiple-Choice Questions.** After reading the corresponding chapter in *The Enduring Vision,* Concise Third Edition, you should try to answer these questions. They are designed to help you to review the significant material in the chapter; they will probably be similar to the kinds of questions and essays that your professor will give you to write on in papers, quizzes, and examinations. Answers to the multiple-choice questions appear at the end of each *Student Guide* chapter.

For help in preparing the *Student Guide,* I would like to thank the editors, Colleen Kyle and Michael Kerns. I am also grateful to my husband, Alan Krumholz, and to my son, Mark, for their patience and support while I worked on this project.

CHAPTER 1
America Begins

Outline

I. **The First Americans**
   A. *Introduction*
      1. Majority of Native Americans descendants of peoples from Siberia who cross land bridge to Alaska about 15,000 years ago
      2. 9,000 years ago, others cross same area and spread over North American continent; ancestors of Apaches and Navajos
      3. 5,000 years ago, Eskimos (Inuits) and Aleuts cross Bering Sea in boats
   B. *The Peopling of North America: The Paleo-Indians*
      1. Paleo-Indians, early hunters, live in small groups
      2. 9000 B.C., mammoths, mastodons, and other big game become extinct because of climate warming and humans' hunting
   C. *Archaic Societies*
      1. Climate warms until 4000 B.C.; warming produces tremendous range of plants and animals in North America
      2. Archaic peoples (native North Americans, 8000 B.C. to 1500 B.C.) able to broaden diet; in East and Midwest larger populations can be sustained in smaller area
      3. Archaic peoples of Midwest and East establish permanent villages; make tools and weapons from stone, bone, shell, clay, leather; start regional networks of trade in products and ideas
      4. Archaic peoples develop gender roles in work: men hunt and fish, women harvest and prepare wild plants

II. **The Indians' Continent**
   A. *The Northern and Western Perimeters*
      1. 1500 B.C., in western Alaska new arctic way of life emerges: Eskimos and Aleuts make and use first bows and arrows, ceramic pottery, pit houses
      2. Eskimos spread across tundra regions as far east as Greenland; trade for metal goods with Norse in Newfoundland in tenth century
      3. Along Pacific coast as far south as northern California, Native Americans fish for salmon; dry and store catch year-round; establish permanent villages

4. Farther south and inland, California Native Americans also reside in permanent villages; sustain themselves by collecting and grinding acorns into meal
5. Both groups engage in trade, warfare; unite under chiefs' leadership
6. Great Basin too dry to support more than small hunting-and-gathering nomadic tribes

B. *The Southwest*
1. 5000 B.C., New World farming begins in central Mexico; spreads to western New Mexico by 3500 B.C.
2. Two new Native American cultures based on agriculture arise in Southwest: Hohokam and Anasazi
3. Hohokams build extensive canal systems for irrigation; reside in permanent villages of several hundred people
4. Anasazis, ancestors of modern Pueblo Indians, dominate Southwest for almost 600 years; found villages such as Chaco Canyon, New Mexico, inhabited by about 15,000 people
5. Prolonged drought in twelfth and thirteenth centuries forces Anasazis and Hohokams to abandon large settlements; break into small groups clustering wherever there is a little water; their cultures decline
6. At same time, foraging Apaches and Navajos enter Southwest

C. *The Eastern Woodlands*
1. Tribes in Eastern Woodlands (Mississippi Valley to Atlantic coast) experiment with village life and political centralization before they farm
2. 1200 B.C., 5,000 people live at Poverty Point on shore of Mississippi River in Louisiana; as Poverty Point declines after three centuries, new mound-building culture, Adena, emerges
3. Adena mounds, often containing graves and having religious significance, built all over the Mississippi Valley and Northeast
4. First century B.C., Adena culture evolves into more complex and widespread Hopewell civilization, which lasts until fifth century A.D.
5. Mississippians (people living on flood plains of the river and its tributaries) become first eastern agriculturalists by seventh century A.D.
6. Mississippian culture incorporates Hopewell and new ideas from Mexico into way of life; features towns with thousands of inhabitants, most important Cahokia (near present-day St. Louis); sophisticated crafts, sun worshipers, centralized political system
7. Unable to raise enough food, Cahokian and Mississippian peoples decline starting thirteenth century; most Eastern Woodlands Indians abandon large settlements, centralized political power
8. 1500 A.D., diverse Native American cultures found in various parts of North America; tribes have in common the use of bows and arrows and ceramic pottery, burial rituals, preference for kin-based communities, rejection of political centralization

III. American Peoples on the Eve of European Contact
A. *Introduction*

1. 1492, 75 million people inhabit Western Hemisphere; 7 to 10 million of them live north of Mexico
2. Sparse population of nomadic tribes found in Great Basin, High Plains, northern forests; more dense population, permanent settlements found on Pacific and Atlantic coasts, in Southwest, Southeast, Mississippi Valley
3. Several hundred tribes and nations with different languages
4. For all tribes, most important social groupings are family, clan, village

B. *Family and Community*
1. Kinship holds Native American societies together
2. Kinship group (or clan) far more important than nuclear family of husband, wife, young children
3. Men hunt, fish, trade, negotiate, fight; women farm (except in Southwest, where both sexes cultivate)

C. *Spiritual and Social Values*
1. All nature, including humanity, interrelated, suffused with spiritual powers (in Algonquian, manitou)
2. Native Americans try to placate, be in tune with spiritual forces: interpret dreams, alter consciousness by acts of physical endurance (questing) and rituals (Sun Dance), seeking advice of shamans
3. Native American communities demand conformity, cooperation, consensus
4. To smooth relations among persons of unequal status and power and to hold society together, Native Americans rely on reciprocity: giving gifts, trading goods in exchange for prestige, deference, authority
5. Indians' view of property based on social reciprocity
6. Indians value order, endurance; fear ghosts, witchcraft

Vocabulary

The following terms are used in Chapter 1. To understand the chapter fully, it is important that you know what each of them means.

indigenous native to a particular region

archaeologist one who scientifically studies any prehistoric culture by excavation and description of its remains

shaman a medicine man; a worker with the supernatural

kiva a large chamber, often wholly or partially underground, in a Pueblo Indian village; used for religious ceremonies and other purposes

deference submission or yielding to the judgment, opinion, and/or free will of another; respectful or courteous regard

clan a group of families or households whose heads claim descent from a common ancestor

Copyright © Houghton Mifflin Company. All rights reserved.

reciprocity a system of mutual give-and-take, allowing individuals or social groups of unequal power, wealth, or status to get along while preserving unequal power relationships; also, a system by which human beings can coexist with nature and the powerful supernatural forces in which they believe

consensus agreement in opinion; collective opinion

Identifications

After reading Chapter 1, you should be able to identify and explain the historical significance of each of the following:

Paleo-Indians

Archaic peoples

pit houses

Hohokam culture

Anasazi and Pueblo cultures

Chaco Canyon

Poverty Point, mound-building culture, and Adena culture

Hopewell and Mississippian cultures

Eastern Woodlands Indians

Cahokia

nuclear families versus extended families

manitou

Skill Building: Maps

On the map of North America, locate the regions where these Native American cultures and the sites associated with them existed:

Aleuts, Eskimos, and arctic culture

Northwest Coast Indians

California Indians

hunting bands of the Great Basin

Hohokam culture

Anasazi and Pueblo cultures

Poverty Point

Adena culture

Hopewell and Mississippian cultures (Cahokia)

Eastern Woodlands culture

Copyright © Houghton Mifflin Company. All rights reserved.

America Begins 5

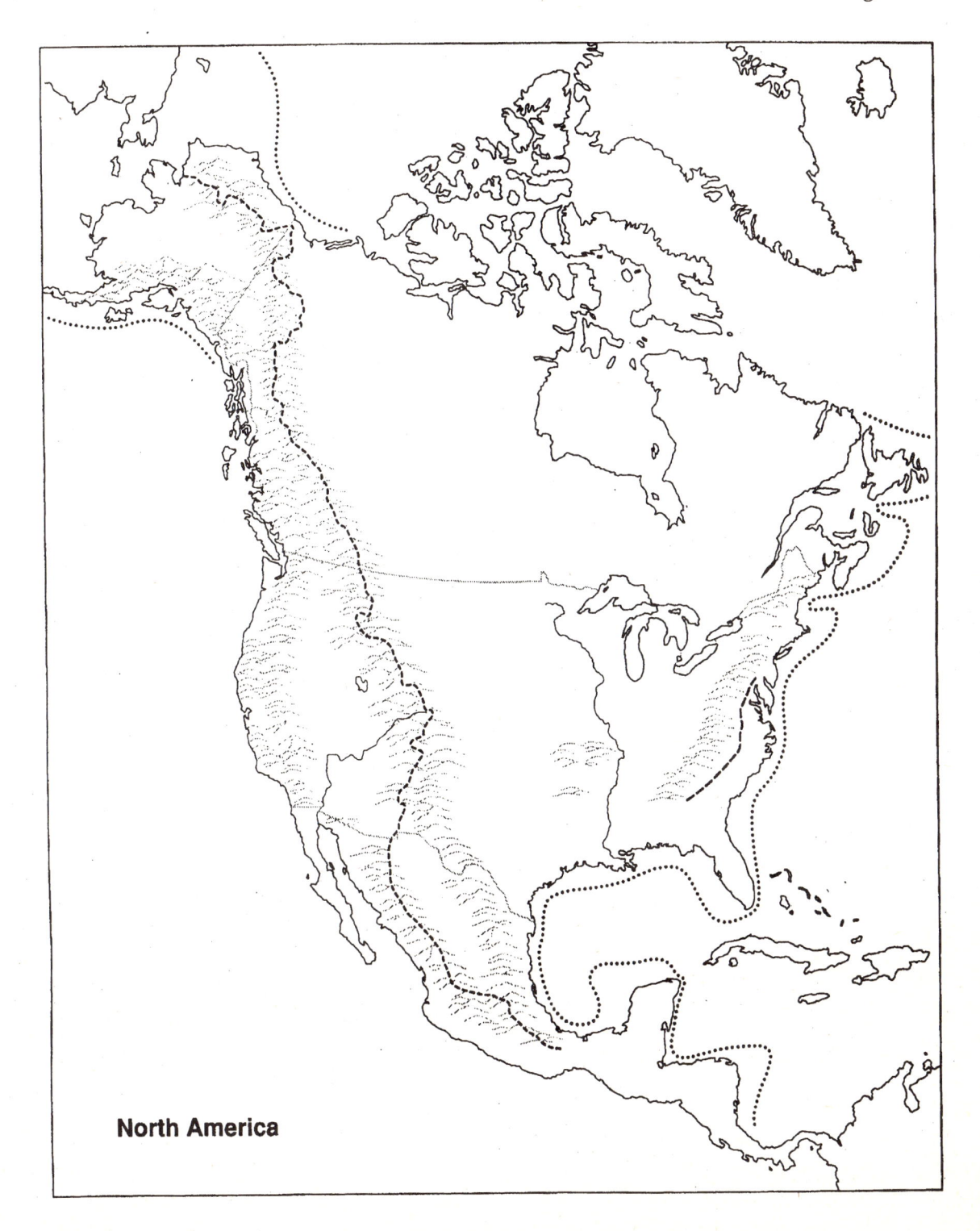

North America

Multiple-Choice Questions

Circle the letter of the item that best completes each statement or answers the question.

1. The majority of American Indians are descended from people who 15,000 years ago
   a. crossed the Atlantic in giant outrigger canoes from the western coast of Africa.
   b. crossed the Atlantic in swift sailing vessels from northern Europe to Iceland to New England.
   c. migrated from Asia across the then-existing Alaska-Siberia land bridge.
   d. migrated in outrigger canoes from Polynesia to the Isthmus of Panama and Central America.

2. The densest Native American populations in what would later be the United States were found
   a. in the Great Basin.
   b. on the High Plains.
   c. on the Pacific coast.
   d. in the northern forests.

3. Which of these Native American cultures is *not* correctly matched to the geographical area in which it flourished?
   a. Pueblo—Arizona and New Mexico
   b. Woodlands—the Pacific Northwest and California
   c. Hopewell—the Midwest
   d. Hohokam—Arizona

4. Which one of these did *not* help to shape Native Americans' social and cultural development before 1500?
   a. geographical isolation
   b. great climatic and geographical variations across America
   c. contact with African cultures, from which Native Americans adopted many practices
   d. long-term changes or cycles in weather, such as warming trends and extended droughts

5. Which of the following tribes was the ancestor of the modern Pueblo Indians?
   a. Adenas
   b. Anasazis
   c. Aleuts
   d. Apaches

6. At the time of Columbus's first voyage to the New World, about how many Native Americans lived on the continent north of present-day Mexico?
   a. 7 million to 10 million
   b. 75 million
   c. 50,000 to 100,000
   d. 1 million to 2 million

7. Which of these characterized Native American culture before contact with the Old World?
   a. the belief that land belonged to and should be used by only the people who lived on it
   b. strong nuclear family ties
   c. the belief that all nature was infused with spiritual power
   d. highly organized nation-states ruled by powerful chiefs

8. Which of the following statements about American Indians is correct?
   a. There is no evidence of any people living in the Americas earlier than 15,000 years ago.
   b. Indians did not know how to build irrigation systems for agriculture until they learned it from the Spanish *conquistadores*.
   c. Indian society frowned on all competitive behavior.
   d. New England tribes allowed women as well as men to serve as chiefs.

9. In which region did Native American men and women both work at farming?
   a. Northeast
   b. Great Basin
   c. Southwest
   d. Mississippi Valley

10. The term *Archaic peoples* refers to
    a. native North Americans from about 8000 to 1500 B.C.
    b. the first nomadic hunters to reach North America.
    c. the mound builders of the Mississippi Valley.
    d. all Native Americans living here at the time of Columbus's voyage.

11. The earliest direct contact between Americans and Europeans probably occurred in about the tenth century A.D. between
    a. the Eastern Woodlands tribes and French explorers.
    b. the Aztecs and the Spanish in Mexico.
    c. the Russians and the Pacific Northwest tribes on the Washington coast.
    d. Eskimos and Norse in Greenland and Newfoundland.

12. Agriculture was first practiced by the Indians of the
    a. Pacific Northwest.
    b. desert Southwest.
    c. midwestern heartland.
    d. Atlantic coast.

Essay Questions

1. Compare and contrast the development and later decline of each of these major Native American cultures: Hohokam and Anasazi; Adena, Hopewell, and Mississippian.

2. Discuss the differing ways of life of the Native Americans living in the Arctic, the Pacific Northwest, California, the Great Basin, the Southwest, the Mississippi Valley, and the Eastern Woodlands. Explain how the physical environment influenced each way of life.

Copyright © Houghton Mifflin Company. All rights reserved.

8 Chapter 1

3. Because the Native Americans of the present-day United States had not developed written languages before the arrival of Europeans, how have historians attempted to reconstruct Native American history? Give as many specific examples from Chapter 1 as possible.

4. Compare and contrast the descriptions of Native American culture presented in Chapter 1 with the impressions offered in movies and television.

Answers to Multiple-Choice Questions

1a. No. There is no evidence for this.
1b. No. No evidence for this.
1c. Yes. See page 2.
1d. No. No evidence for this.

2a. No. Too dry to sustain dense population.
2b. No. Climate unfavorable for high density.
2c. Yes. Climate and resources made this possible. See page 6.
2d. No. Climate unfavorable for high density.

3a. No. The Pueblos did live in Arizona and New Mexico.
3b. Yes. The Woodlands culture should not be matched with the Pacific Northwest and California. It existed from the Mississippi River to the Atlantic Coast. See page 7.
3c. No. Hopewell culture was associated with the Midwest.
3d. No. Hohokam culture was found in Arizona.

4a. No. Geographical isolation was important in shaping Indian social and cultural development prior to 1500.
4b. No. Climatic and geographical variations were major determinants of culture.
4c. Yes. This did not help shape Native American development because there is no evidence of any contact before 1500.
4d. No. Weather cycles played a major role in shaping Indian cultures.

5a. No. They inhabited the Ohio Valley, not the Southwest of the Pueblo people.
5b. Yes. See pages 6–7.
5c. No. They spread from Alaska across Canada.
5d. No. Apaches came into the Southwest after the Pueblo peoples.

6a. Yes. See page 10.
6b. No. That is how many lived in all of the Western Hemisphere.
6c. No. Number much too small.
6d. No. Number is low.

7a. No. Tribes often shared use of land with others for different purposes.
7b. No. Extended family and clan were more important than nuclear family ties.
7c. Yes. See page 11.
7d. No. In the few areas where centralized states and powerful chiefs had existed, changing ecological conditions undermined them.

8a. No. Archaeologists have found evidence of earlier habitation.
8b. No. Native Americans in the Southwest built extensive irrigation systems before they had contact with the Spanish.
8c. No. Many tribes engaged in highly competitive games.
8d. Yes. See page 10.

9a. No. Only women.
9b. No. No farming there.
9c. Yes. See page 10.
9d. No. Only women.

10a. Yes. See page 3.
10b. No. They are called Paleo-Indians.
10c. No. They came later.
10d. No. They belonged to many different regional cultures and tribes at the time of Columbus's voyage.

11a. No. The French came much later.
11b. No. The Spanish came much later.
11c. No. The Russians came much later.
11d. Yes. See page 4.

12a. No. They were able to sustain themselves by fishing and gathering.
12b. Yes. Agriculture first spread to tribes in the Southwest from central Mexican tribes.
12c. No. They came to agriculture later.
12d. No. They came to agriculture later.

CHAPTER 2
Transatlantic Encounters and Colonial Beginnings, 1492–1630

Outline

I. **African and European Peoples**
   A. *Mediterranean Crossroads*
      1. Mediterranean Sea serves since ancient times as crossroads for trade and exchange of religious and political ideas among Africans, Asians, and Europeans
      2. Seventh to fourteenth centuries Muslim conquerors spread Islam to Southeast Asia, West Africa, and southern Europe
      3. Christians carry their religion to central and northern Europe
      4. Eleventh century religious wars between Christians and Muslims begin; Christian Crusaders try to drive Islam out of Europe and Middle East; Muslims declare holy war against Christians
      5. By 1492, Christian Spain drives Muslims out of Iberian peninsula
      6. Portugal begins series of voyages of discovery in 1400s down African coast to dominate gold and other trade with West Africa
   B. *West Africa and Its Peoples*
      1. Before Portugal opens Atlantic route, trade between sub-Saharan Africa and Europe carried on by land caravans across the Sudan; this trade stimulates rise of powerful Savanna (Grassland) kingdoms: Ghana, Mali (Timbuktu, its main city, center of trade and Islamic learning), and Songhai, between eleventh and fifteenth centuries
      2. When European nations adopt gold standard in fifteenth century, West Coast African states: Senegambia, Guinea, Benin, arise to become main supplier of gold to Europe
      3. Savanna emperors claim semidivine status; West African society built around kinship groups. Their extended family tradition helps enslaved Africans in America survive the break-up of nuclear families by slavery. Africans do not regard land as saleable commodity, are very religious, believe in spirit world, ancestor worship, witchcraft
      4. West Africans engage in agriculture; principal crops, yams and rice
      5. West Africans develop sophisticated art and music; much twentieth-century art and jazz based on African forms
      6. 1500, Islam starting to spread to common people of grasslands; Christianity makes

few inroads until nineteenth century
- C. *European Culture and Society*
    1. 1492, Europe at height of Renaissance; scholars trying to map world, understand astronomy
    2. European society hierarchical; at top, kings rule. To lessen their dependence on luxury-loving nobility, kings turning increasingly to rising middle class of bankers and merchants for financial support; at bottom, peasants comprise 80 percent of population, are heavily taxed
    3. Population increases in Europe in sixteenth and seventeenth centuries make land scarce and valuable; upper classes enclose common fields and claim them as their private property; masses of impoverished, displaced peasants drift to towns or wander countryside looking for work
    4. Traditional European society (based on extended family, social reciprocity, regulated economic practices) breaking down
    5. Patriarchal nuclear families replacing kinship networks; new business forms and practices disregard social reciprocity; merchants demand unfettered competition and acquisition of wealth
- D. *Religious Upheavals*
    1. Christian majority and small Jewish and Muslim minorities of sixteenth-century Europe monotheistic; many Europeans also believe in magic and witchcraft, like Africans and Native Americans of their time
    2. Until 1517, Roman Catholic Church (headed by pope and administered by hierarchy of clergy, who do not marry) exercises authority almost everywhere in Europe
    3. By fifteenth century, Church sells indulgences (blessings to shorten repentant sinners' time in purgatory) in exchange for donations to the Church
    4. In 1517 Martin Luther denounces indulgences and other corrupt practices, breaks with pope, initiates Protestant Reformation
    5. Luther and other Protestants preach person cannot buy or earn salvation by good works (or donations); God alone decides who is saved, who damned; Christians must have faith in God's love and justice
    6. John Calvin and his followers emphasize doctrine of predestination (God's assigning majority of sinful human beings to hell; only a few saved by God's grace for heaven)
    7. Catholic Church responds with Counter-Reformation; cleans out corruption, attempts to suppress Protestantism
    8. European countries divide into rival Protestant and Catholic camps
    9. Protestantism encourages literacy and education and makes the individual responsible for his or her own spiritual and moral condition
    10. Reformation and Counter-Reformation create in Europeans crusading spirit and sense of superiority, justifying conquest and exploitation of non-Christians in Africa and North America
- E. *The Rise of Puritanism in England*
    1. English King Henry VIII wants pope to annul his marriage to Catherine of Aragon,

who has not produced male heir
2. When pope refuses (1533–1534), Henry proclaims himself head of separate Church of England (Anglican Church); seizes and sells property of Catholic Church in England
3. Religious strife continues in England for more than one hundred years after Henry VIII breaks with Catholic Church
4. King Edward VI (Henry's son) leans toward Protestantism; Queen Mary (Henry's daughter) tries to restore Catholicism by burning Protestants at stake
5. Mary's successor and half-sister Elizabeth I and majority of English people react by turning against Catholicism
6. English differ on how Protestant the Anglican Church should be; English Calvinists (Puritans) want to remove all vestiges of Catholicism, emphasize predestination, believe only the saved should belong to the church, bishops should be eliminated
7. Puritanism, with theme of self-discipline, appeals particularly to English middle class
8. Most early New England settlers come from these middle-class Puritans
9. After Elizabeth's death religious tensions in England escalate; Stuart kings, James I (1603–1625) and Charles I (1625–1649), crack down on Nonseparatist Puritans, trying to reform Anglican Church from within, and Separatist Puritans, who wish to establish congregations outside Church of England
10. Economic hard times hit England in 1600s; under impact of economic woes and religious persecution, group of Separatists go to Holland and later found Plymouth in New England; Nonseparatists obtain charter (1628–1629) for another colony, Massachusetts Bay, and other Nonseparatists later settle Connecticut

II. European Expansion
   A. Seaborne Expansion
   1. In mid-fifteenth century, improved maritime technology (caravel, compass, astrolabe) and better mapmaking facilitate European seaborne expansion
   2. Portugal, under Prince Henry "the Navigator," leads the way
   3. Portuguese sailors push down west coast of Africa, establish slave station at Arguin, round Cape of Good Hope, develop commercial links with India
   4. These voyages bring Europeans into contact with black Africans

   B. The "New Slavery" and Racism
   1. Slavery exists in West Africa before Europeans arrive; not based on racial difference between master and slave
   2. First, Muslims from north, and then Europeans, turn African slavery into intercontinental business
   3. European slavers buy war captives from African slave-trading kings
   4. By nineteenth century, nearly 12 million Africans shipped across Atlantic to labor under brutal conditions on plantations in New World
   5. Profits made in slave trade fuel commercial expansion of Europe
   6. Europeans justify slavery by seeing black Africans as not only culturally and

physically different, but subhuman
- C. *Europeans Reach America*
    1. 1492, Spain's Isabella and Ferdinand finance Christopher Columbus's first voyage
    2. Columbus lands on San Salvador; makes three later voyages; establishes Spanish colonies; does not realize he has discovered New World
    3. England's Henry VII sends John Cabot across northern Atlantic; Cabot claims Nova Scotia and Newfoundland for England
    4. 1507, Europeans realize new lands have been discovered, give them name *America*
    5. Voyages thereafter mostly have purpose to find way past America to Asia: 1513, Vasco Núñez de Balboa crosses isthmus of Panama, Ferdinand Magellan sails around southern tip of South America
    6. Giovanni da Verrazano and Jacques Cartier look for "northwest passage" to Asia
- D. *Spain's Conquistadores*
    1. Early Spanish explorers, including Columbus, become conquerors as well
    2. Columbus exports Native American slaves and gives land grants to Spaniards with right to forced labor of Native Americans living on the land
    3. 1519–1521, Hernán Cortés lands in Mexico and conquers mighty Aztec empire
    4. During rest of sixteenth century, Spanish conquerors fan out over Caribbean and the Americas from Mexico to Chile, subduing and enslaving native peoples
    5. Native American population nearly decimated by European diseases to which they have no immunity; to replace dying Native American slaves, Portuguese deliver African slaves
- E. *The Columbian Exchange*
    1. "Columbian exchange" among Europe, Africa, America produces greater and more varied food supply; this leads to huge population growth in Europe
    2. Spain's empire sees much racial mixing as almost 300,000 Spanish male settlers father children of African and Indian women
    3. New World's sugar, livestock, and silver greatly enrich Spain, but riches poorly handled by Spanish monarchy, benefiting country little in long-run

III. Footholds in North America
- A. *New Spain's Northern Frontier*
    1. During 1500s, Spanish search for gold, silver, and slaves penetrates parts of future United States
    2. Juan Ponce de León, Florida; Cabeza de Vaca, New Mexico; Francisco Vásquez de Coronado and Hérnan de Soto, South, Midwest, and Southwest
    3. 1565, Spain founds first successful settlement on mainland future United States—St. Augustine, Florida
    4. 1598, Spain starts royal colony of New Mexico; 1609, Santa Fe established
- B. *France: Initial Failures and Canadian Success*

14 *Chapter 2*

   1. 1541, Jacques Cartier builds fort on Indian land in St. Lawrence Valley; alienates Indians
   2. French attempts at planting permanent colonies in St. Lawrence Valley (1541), South Carolina (1562), Florida (1564) all fail

C. *The Enterprising Dutch*
   1. 1609, Henry Hudson explores for the Dutch the river that bears his name today
   2. 1614, Dutch build Fort Nassau (on site of today's Albany, New York) to trade with Native Americans for furs
   3. 1625, Dutch found New Amsterdam on Manhattan Island, and Peter Minuit buys the island from Native Americans

D. *Elizabethan England and the Wider World*
   1. In late 1500s England becomes interested in the New World
   2. With encouragement of Queen Elizabeth, English "sea dogs" (Francis Drake and others) raid Spanish treasure ships and ports, search for northwest passage and for colony sites
   3. 1587, Sir Walter Raleigh sponsors colony on Roanoke Island; colonists disappear
   4. English government not interested in putting money into colony founding; private groups (using joint-stock companies) and individuals take the initiative in colonization

E. *The Beginnings of English Colonization: Virginia*
   1. 1606, Virginia Company of London receives charter from King James I; 1607, company ships 105 settlers to Jamestown
   2. Settlers refuse to farm, hunting for gold instead; starve, revert to anarchy; Captain John Smith imposes discipline, saves colony; he also establishes good relations with Native Americans
   3. John Rolfe's tobacco provides cash crop that ensures Virginia's economic success
   4. To attract settlers and capital, company institutes headright system; planters accumulate large estates by importing indentured servants
   5. 1619, company grants settlers right to elect a legislative assembly, the House of Burgesses; start of representative government in North America
   6. 1622–1625, major Indian wars in Virginia
   7. 1624, James I revokes Virginia Company charter, settlement becomes royal colony

F. *The Origins of New England: Plymouth Plantation*
   1. 1620, *Mayflower* lands 102 English men and women at Plymouth, Massachusetts
   2. Settlement financed by group of English merchants who hold patent from Virginia Company
   3. About half of settlers are English Separatists, who had been living in Holland; rest, other English citizens
   4. Settlers agree to send lumber, furs, fish to English merchants to repay their investment

5. Winter storms blow *Mayflower* off course; colonists land outside boundaries of Virginia and jurisdiction of its government
6. Adult males sign Mayflower Compact establishing colony of Plymouth Plantation and their own civil government and pledging to abide by its laws
7. Half of the Pilgrims die during first winter at Plymouth; survivors helped by two friendly Native Americans, Squanto and Samoset
8. Later relations between Plymouth settlers and neighboring Native Americans deteriorate
9. Plymouth's importance: shapes our image of sturdy, freedom-seeking English colonists; foreshadows coercive behavior toward Native Americans employed later by English settlers; is vanguard of mighty Puritan migration to New England in 1630s

Vocabulary

The following terms are used in Chapter 2. To understand the chapter fully, it is important that you know what each of them means.

savanna tropical grassland

monotheistic pertaining to belief in only one god (as opposed to **polytheistic,** having to do with belief in and worship of many gods)

hierarchy a system of placing persons or things in a graded order, from lowest to highest in wealth, power, status, and so on

sumptuary laws laws regulating personal habits that offend the moral or religious conscience of the community

capitalism a system under which the means of production, distribution, and exchange are in large measure privately owned and directed, and in which prices and wages are determined by supply-and-demand market forces

gentry landowners with substantial amounts of property and without aristocratic titles; considered "gentlemen" and therefore not to do manual labor; played an important role in English government

caravel a type of small, maneuverable ship developed by the Spanish and Portuguese in the 1400s

astrolabe an astronomical instrument for taking the altitude of the sun or stars, useful in solving problems in astronomy and navigation

patent an official document conferring a right (such as the exclusive right to make use of or sell an invention) or a grant of land (such as the charter given by the Virginia Company to Thomas Weston and other merchants)

Identifications

After reading Chapter 2, you should be able to identify and explain the historical significance of each of the following:

English "Poor Laws"
enclose (enclosure movement)
joint-stock company
indulgences, Martin Luther, and the Protestant Reformation
John Calvin and the doctrine of predestination
Counter-Reformation
Puritans versus Anglicans
conversion experience, "saints," and the "elect"
Prince Henry "the Navigator"
Vasco da Gama
Vasco Núñez de Balboa
Ferdinand Magellan
northwest passage
conquistadores and *encomiendas*
Hernán Cortés
Juan Ponce de León, Cabeza de Vaca, Hérnan de Soto, Francisco Coronado
Francis Drake, Walter Raleigh
Elizabeth I and James I
Virginia Company of London
Captain John Smith
John Rolfe
headrights
Peter Minuit
Separatists
Thomas Weston, Pilgrims, and Plymouth Plantation
Mayflower Compact

Skill Building: Maps

1. On the map of Africa, locate each of the following and explain its historical significance:
    Sahara Desert
    Ghana
    Mali
    Songhai
    Timbuktu

Benin

Guinea

Senegambia

Arguin

the Equator

Cape of Good Hope

2. On the map of Central and South America, locate each of the following places and explain which European explorer and conqueror is associated with it:

San Salvador

Hispaniola (Haiti and the Dominican Republic)

isthmus of Panama

Caribbean Sea

Pacific Ocean

Atlantic Ocean

Strait of Magellan

Tenochtitlán (Mexico City)

Puerto Rico

3. On the map of North America, locate each of the following and indicate which European country had claimed and/or settled it by 1625:

Great Lakes

Chesapeake Bay

Mississippi River

Great Plains

Newfoundland

Acadia (Nova Scotia)

Santa Fe

St. Lawrence River

St. Augustine, Florida

Jamestown, Virginia

Quebec

18 *Chapter 2*

Fort Nassau (later Albany, New York)

New Amsterdam (later New York City)

Roanoke Island (off the coast of North Carolina)

Plymouth Plantation

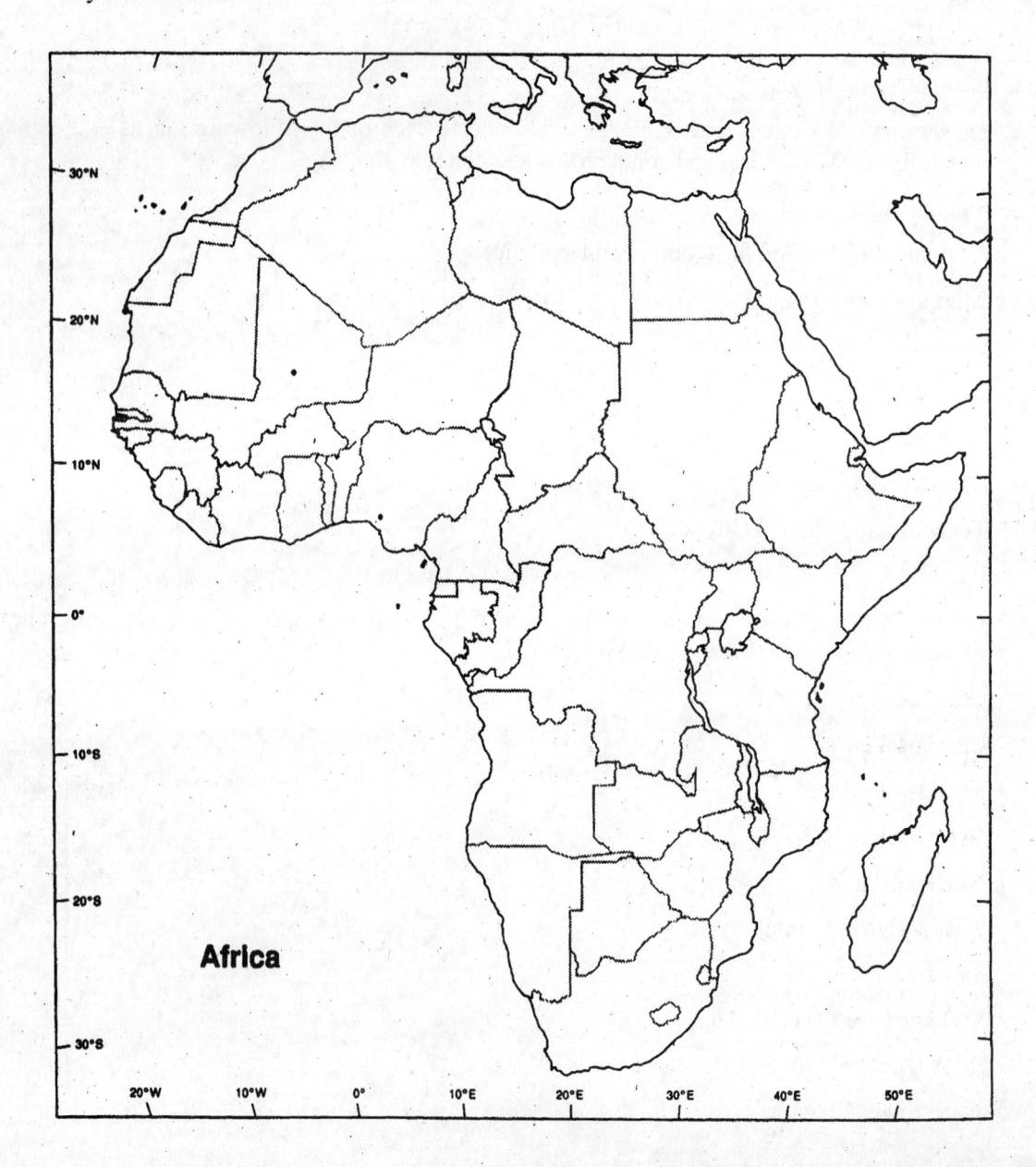

Africa

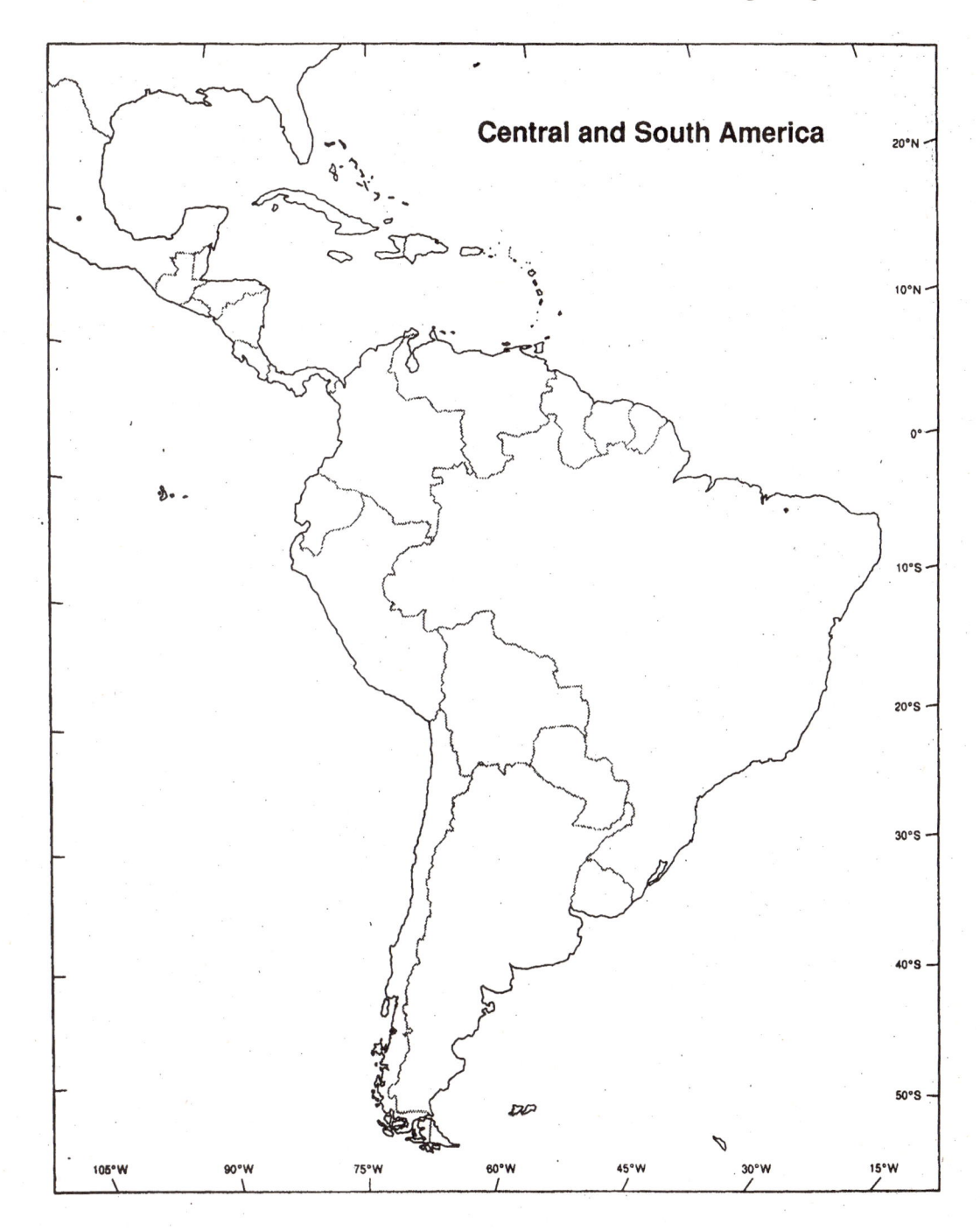

Transatlantic Encounters and Colonial Beginnings, 1492–1630 19

Central and South America

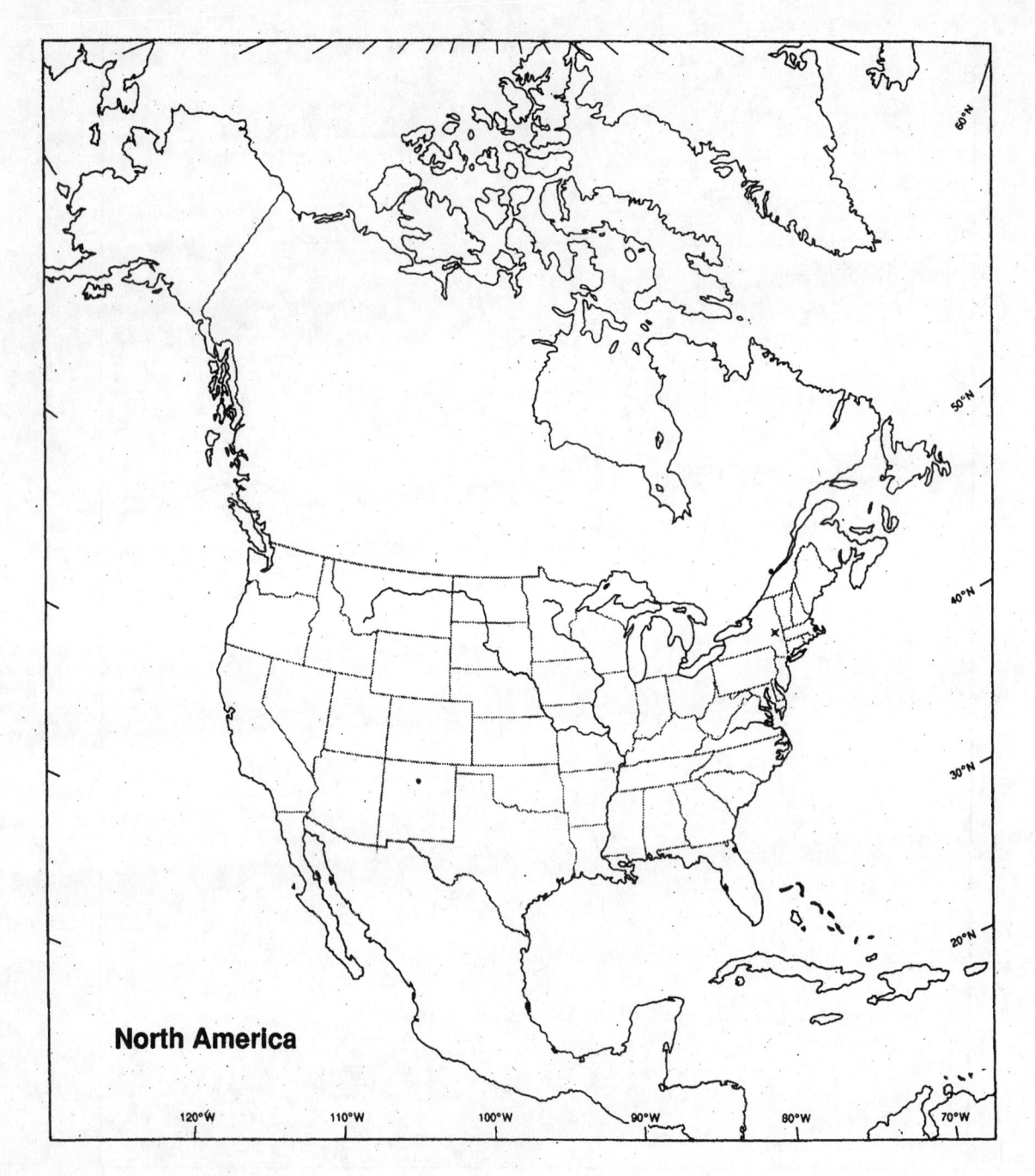

North America

Multiple-Choice Questions

Circle the letter of the item that best completes each statement or answers the question.

1. By the 1500s the nuclear family unit was becoming increasingly important among
   a. western Europeans.
   b. South American Indians.
   c. North American Indians.
   d. West Africans.

2. The beginnings of representative government in the European settlements in North America can be found in
   a. the Spanish colony at St. Augustine, Florida.
   b. Dutch New Netherlands, where the inhabitants were granted the right to elect their own legislature in the colony's charter.
   c. Virginia, when, in 1619, the company provided for the inhabitants' election of an assembly.
   d. 1609, in Santa Fe, when the Spanish created a legislature to attract more settlers.

3. Which of the following statements about West African society at the time of first contact with Europeans is correct?
   a. Slavery was unknown in West Africa.
   b. The majority of West Africans were either Muslims or Christians.
   c. Agriculture had not yet developed. The majority of West Africans were hunters and gatherers.
   d. Kinship groups were important; men made a payment to their brides' kin at the time of marriage.

4. The financing of the Virginia settlement came from
   a. the English government.
   b. a joint-stock company.
   c. the Church of England.
   d. all of the above

5. The primary economic activity in the Dutch colony of New Netherland was
   a. farming.
   b. logging and shipbuilding.
   c. fur trading.
   d. fishing.

6. The first Europeans to develop the intercontinental African slave trade were
   a. English.
   b. French.
   c. Italian.
   d. Portuguese.

Copyright © Houghton Mifflin Company. All rights reserved.

22 *Chapter 2*

7. The primary aim of the explorations of Balboa, Magellan, Verrazano, and Cartier was to find
   a. a water passage through the Americas and reach Asia.
   b. the fabled fountain of youth.
   c. the Seven Cities of Gold.
   d. favorable places for their respective nations to plant new colonies.

8. Which of the following statements about England's Queen Elizabeth I is correct?
   a. During her reign English armies used brutal methods to suppress Irish rebellion.
   b. She tried to suppress the raids of the English "sea dogs" on Spanish ports in order to avoid war.
   c. She invested substantial sums of government money in the planting of English North American settlements like Roanoke and Jamestown.
   d. She eagerly embraced Puritanism.

9. Which of the following statements about English Puritans is correct?
   a. Their views were closer to Catholicism than Protestantism.
   b. They believed that only those who had had a conversion experience and knew they were saved should be allowed to join the congregation.
   c. They were mostly from the English aristocracy.
   d. They rejected the doctrine of predestination in favor of the more democratic belief that all humans are capable of earning salvation.

10. Who of the following is *incorrectly* matched with his deeds?
    a. Hernán Cortés—conquered the Aztecs, built Mexico City
    b. Francisco Coronado—found the Grand Canyon, plundered the New Mexico pueblos
    c. Giovanni da Verrazano—founded Quebec, sent *coureurs de bois* to live with the Native Americans
    d. Jacques Cartier—explored the St. Lawrence River, made an early French attempt to colonize North America

Essay Questions

1. Compare and contrast the founding and early development of Virginia and Plymouth. Given that both were English colonies, how do you account for the differences?

2. "During the first third of the seventeenth century, the general outlines of European claims in North America emerged, as did the basic elements of the various colonies' economic life." Discuss this statement with reference to the Spanish, French, Dutch, and English colonies in North America.

3. Discuss the religious and political conflicts and the economic conditions in sixteenth- and early-seventeenth-century England that made the English interested in New World exploration and colonization.

4. "The displacement of Indians and the enslavement of Africans tarnished the early history of European settlement in the New World." Illustrate this statement by discussing the African

Transatlantic Encounters and Colonial Beginnings, 1492–1630

slave trade and relations between the Spanish, French, Dutch, and English settlers and the various Native American peoples.

5. Discuss the concept of social reciprocity. How did it operate in Native American, West African, and traditional European societies? In what ways was it breaking down in western Europe by the sixteenth and seventeenth centuries?

Answers to Multiple-Choice Questions

1a. Yes. See page 19.
1b. No. For Indians the extended family, clan, and tribe were more important than the nuclear family.
1c. No. Same as 1b.
1d. No. West Africans valued extended family ties.

2a. No. The Spanish did not grant representative legislative bodies to their colonies.
2b. No. The Dutch did not make such a promise.
2c. Yes. See page 32.
2d. No. Same as in 2a.

3a. No. Slavery was practiced in West Africa, but it was not based on race.
3b. No. The majority practiced religions indigenous to the region.
3c. No. West Africans were mainly farmers, growing rice, yams, and other crops.
3d. Yes. See pages 14–18.

4a. No. The English government gave no financial backing to colonial settlements until the last mainland one in Georgia.
4b. Yes. The Virginia Company of London. See page 31.
4c. No. The Anglican Church did not fund colonies.
4d. No. See 4a and 4c.

5a. No. Most farming was to feed themselves, not for commercial export.
5b. No. Not big industries in New Netherlands.
5c. Yes. The Dutch traded with the Indians to obtain beaver and other pelts for export. See page 29.
5d. No. Not a big commercial activity yet.

6a. No. They would not dominate the international slave trade until the eighteenth century.
6b. No. They were rather minor players.
6c. No. Same as 6b.
6d. Yes. See page 23.

7a. Yes. See page 25.
7b. No. That was a motivation for Ponce de León.
7c. No. That was a motivation for Coronado.
7d. No. That was less important than finding the water passage to Asia.

8a. Yes. See page 29. Many of these same brutal tactics the English would later use against North American Indians.
8b. No. She encouraged them and shared in the plunder.
8c. No. She spent all the government's funds on the Irish war and fighting the Spanish.
8d. No. She was never comfortable with Puritanism and preferred the Anglican worship.

9a. No. They wanted to rid the Church of England of all vestiges of Catholicism.

Copyright © Houghton Mifflin Company. All rights reserved.

9b. Yes. See page 21.
9c. No. They were mostly from the English middle class.
9d. No. They were firm believers in predestination.

10a. No. Cortés is correctly identified as the conqueror of the Aztecs.
10b. No. Coronado is correctly matched with his deeds.
10c. Yes. Verrazano did not found Quebec.
10d. No. Cartier is correctly matched with his deeds.

CHAPTER 3
Expansion and Diversity: The Rise of Colonial America

Outline

I. **The New England Way**
   A. *A City upon a Hill*
      1. 1630, 700 Puritans arrive in Massachusetts Bay Colony; they bring their charter and governors with them, making Massachusetts largely self-governing
      2. 1630, John Winthrop's sermon, "A Model of Christian Charity," says Puritans will create a godly community, "a city upon a hill" that will serve as example for sinful England to emulate
      3. Puritans want to regain sense of community and social reciprocity fast disappearing in England
   B. *Development of a Puritan Orthodoxy*
      1. Though claiming to be part of Church of England, Massachusetts ignores authority of Anglican bishops; each congregation self-governed by male members (saints), guided by its minister
      2. Only the saved can be church members, but all must attend services and pay taxes to support church; thus Massachusetts has an "established church"
      3. Because literacy and learned clergy essential to salvation, Massachusetts passes Old Deluder (Satan) Act (1647) and founds Harvard College (1636)
      4. New England only part of English colonies in seventeenth century with college-educated elite
   C. *Dissenting Puritans*
      1. Some Puritans dissent from the "New England Way"
      2. Roger Williams preaches that church and state should be separate, and government must not interfere with private religious beliefs or compel church attendance
      3. Massachusetts authorities banish Williams because they believe purpose of government is to protect the true religion and prevent heresy
      4. Williams flees southward, buys land from Native Americans, establishes Rhode Island (1647), only New England colony to practice religious tolerance and separate church and state

5. Massachusetts expels Anne Hutchinson for challenging clerical authority; she and many of her Antinomian followers settle in Rhode Island
6. Some Puritan merchants object to Massachusetts government's attempts to limit their profits and interfere with market economy

D. Power to the Saints
1. In Massachusetts Bay Colony, male church members (saints) eligible to vote for governor and delegates to legislative body (General Court); about 55 percent of adult males can vote
2. Basic unit of local government, the town meeting, open to participation by all male taxpayers
3. New Englanders live in tightly clustered villages; everyone within walking distance of meetinghouse
4. Each family receives land to farm in fields or strips surrounding the town
5. Compact settlements promote social reciprocity, community interaction; allow Puritans to watch each other and enforce godly conduct; Puritan women play important role in building community, enforcing conformity

E. Puritan Families
1. Nuclear family is foundation of Puritan society; wife, children, servants expected to obey husband-father
2. Marriage a civil contract, not a sacrament; divorce legal but rare
3. Courts and churches intervene to keep order and harmony within families
4. Puritans follow English common law giving wife no property rights independent of husband
5. Better living conditions in New England result in longer life expectancy than in England
6. Even sex ratio, rapid natural increase
7. Not possible to get rich from agriculture in New England; seeking better opportunities, Puritans turn to lumbering, fishing, rum distilling, shipbuilding, commerce; as they prosper, become more profit motivated, less preoccupied with religion

F. The Demise of the Puritan Errand
1. Restoration of Stuart kings (1660) dooms Puritan hopes that Church of England will follow New England example
2. In New England, mission also faltering as founders fail to pass on their religious zeal to second and third generations
3. Declining church membership necessitates compromises such as Half-Way Covenant (1662)

G. Expansion and Native Americans
1. Native Americans of coastal New England decimated by disease, initially offer little resistance to Puritan settlement
2. As English push into Connecticut River valley, Pequots object

3. Puritans wage bloody war against Pequots; exterminate whole Pequot village at Mystic, Connecticut; Pequot resistance broken by 1637, way open for Puritan colonization in Connecticut
4. As settlers increase and prosper, Native American population declines
5. European diseases kill off Native Americans; Europeans cut down forests, destroy Native Americans' hunting and gathering areas, reduce Native Americans' food supply
6. Native American population falls from 125,000 in 1600 to 10,000 by 1675; demoralized Native Americans turn to alcohol; others convert to Christianity, consent to live in Puritans' "praying towns"
7. Wampanoag chief Metacom (King Philip) unites Native Americans in last-ditch effort to oust the English (1675–1676)
8. Metacom and thousands of other Native Americans killed; others sold into slavery; Native American population reduced by 40 percent; end of Native American resistance in New England

H. *Economics, Gender, and Satan in Salem*

1. New Englanders become more materialistic, individualistic; sense of community breaks down; economic inequality grows
2. Tensions caused by these changes help to explain Salem witchcraft hysteria (1691–1692); Salem Village's community-oriented farmers accuse Salem Town's prosperous merchants and their wives of witchcraft
3. Twenty people convicted of witchcraft and executed, hundreds more jailed; 1693, governor orders end to trials and release of remaining prisoners
4. Loss of Massachusetts charter (1684) and colony's absorption into Dominion of New England (1686) also contribute to tension
5. By 1700 New Englanders changing from Puritans to Yankees

II. Chesapeake Society

A. *State and Church in Virginia*

1. 1619, Virginia Company of London grants settlers right to elect a representative assembly; after Virginia becomes royal colony, King Charles I (1628) allows continuation of House of Burgesses
2. 1650s, assembly becomes bicameral legislature: elected House of Burgesses, appointed Governor's Council
3. Local government officials in Virginia appointed, not elected
4. Anglican Church established; all Virginians taxed to support it
5. Virginians less religious than New Englanders

B. *Virginia's First Families*

1. Beginning in 1660 Virginia develops an elite upper class
2. Most of elite hail from English merchant families who arrive with capital and become planters

3. They control Royal Council and through their public offices enrich themselves with additional land grants
4. "First Families of Virginia" include Byrds, Lees, Randolphs; they dominate Virginia politics for two centuries.

C. *Maryland*
1. First proprietary colony; founded by Cecilius Calvert (Lord Baltimore)
2. Lord Baltimore wants to create haven for persecuted English Catholics; more Protestants than Catholics settle in Maryland
3. 1649, to protect Catholic minority, Baltimore drafts Act of Religious Toleration; 1654, Protestant majority repeals act, bars Catholics from voting

D. *Tobacco Shapes a Way of Life*
1. Chesapeake life shaped by tobacco growing, the main occupation
2. Population is spread out on farms and plantations near rivers
3. Few commercial centers or towns develop; ships from England come directly to riverfront docks of planters; sell European goods, buy tobacco
4. Planters serve as middlemen for surrounding small farmers; no merchants
5. 1630–1700, 110,000 English arrive; majority as indentured servants to labor on tobacco plantations

E. *Mortality, Gender, and Kinship*
1. Slow population growth in Virginia and Maryland because of scarcity of women, high death rate
2. Life expectancy in 1600s: twenty years fewer in Chesapeake than in New England
3. By early 1700s, mortality down, sex ratio evened out, population growing

F. *Tobacco's Troubles*
1. Increasing economic inequality in Virginia and Maryland; big planters with huge estates exploit labor of indentured servants
2. 1660, tobacco prices fall 50 percent; upward mobility impossible for former indentured servants
3. Servants form frustrated, landless underclass

G. *Bacon's Rebellion*
1. Depressed tobacco prices, resentments of small farmers and landless former servants toward wealthy lead to Bacon's Rebellion
2. Frontier farmers, led by Nathaniel Bacon, fight unauthorized war against Native Americans, 1676
3. Royal governor tries to restrain farmers; they revolt, burn Jamestown, loot plantations of wealthy
4. Bacon dies; rebels disperse

H. *Slavery*
1. 1619, Africans first arrive in Virginia; treated as indentured servants initially
2. 1640–1660, status of Africans deteriorates to that of lifelong slavery

3. After 1660 Chesapeake colonies recognize institution of slavery with laws that define condition and rigidly control blacks
4. Significant numbers of African slaves imported after 1680; 1700, almost 20,000 slaves in Chesapeake colonies
5. Growth of slavery eases intrawhite tensions as whites unite to control African slaves

III. **The Spread of Slavery: The Caribbean and Carolina**
  A. *Introduction*
  1. In 1600s, 40,000 Englishmen settle in West Indies
  2. English West Indies influence English mainland colonies
  3. West Indies important market for New England foodstuffs; West Indies lead way in plantation-slave economy, later copied in mainland South
  4. After 1660, many English West Indians move to Chesapeake and Carolina
  B. *Sugar and Slaves*
  1. Tobacco first export of British West Indies
  2. Sugar cane more profitable crop; planters with enough capital to invest in land, equipment, and African slaves switch to growing it
  3. Sugar planters become wealthy, monopolize best land; many poorer whites move on to Carolina
  4. Sugar planters import so many African slaves that by 1713, blacks outnumber whites by four to one
  C. *Carolina: The First Restoration Colony*
  1. 1663, England's Charles II gives Carolina to some English supporters
  2. Proprietors organize territory into two districts; create bicameral legislature for each
  3. Proprietors adopt headright system to attract settlers
  4. Fundamental Constitutions of Carolina, drawn up by Anthony Ashley Cooper and John Locke, ignored by settlers
  5. North Carolinians mostly small farmers; raise livestock; export tobacco, lumber, pitch
  6. After 1690 South Carolina planters turn to rice cultivation; become only mainland elite as wealthy as West Indies sugar planters
  7. Planters import so many slaves that South Carolina becomes only mainland colony with black majority
  8. 1696, South Carolina adopts brutal slave code copied from Barbados
  9. South Carolina planters also enslave Native Americans and ship them to West Indies; these policies provoke war with Tuscaroras (1711–1713) and Yamasees (1715); Native Americans crushed
  10. 1729, proprietary rule ends; North and South Carolina become royal colonies

IV. **The Middle Colonies**
  A. *Precursors: New Netherland and New Sweden*
  1. Dutch New Netherland becomes North America's first multiethnic society; its

population includes Dutch, Germans, French, Scandinavians, Africans (free and slave), Protestants, Catholics, Jews, Muslims; eighteen different languages spoken there
   2. Dutch get along well with Iroquois (with whom they trade for furs); fight brutal wars against nearby tribes
   3. 1655, New Netherland governor Peter Stuyvesant takes over and annexes fur-trading settlement in lower Delaware valley, founded earlier by Swedes
B. *English Conquests: New York and the Jerseys*
   1. 1664, England's Charles II presents seized Dutch colony New Netherland to his brother, James, Duke of York, who renames it New York
   2. Dutch inhabitants remain, but immigration reduces their portion of New York population to only 44 percent by 1700
   3. 1685, James becomes king; makes New York a royal colony
   4. British royal governors reward loyal followers with big land grants; these patroons grow almost as wealthy as South Carolina rice planters
   5. Another part of captured New Netherland is turned into the Jerseys and given to a group of English proprietors to govern
   6. Jersey settlers (a mixture of English Quakers, Puritans, and Anglicans, Scottish Presbyterians, and Dutch Calvinists) quarrel with each other and the proprietors
   7. 1702, king takes over from proprietors and New Jersey becomes royal colony
C. *Quaker Pennsylvania*
   1. 1681, Charles II gives grant of land in America to William Penn
   2. Penn seeks to found "holy experiment" based on Quaker principles; wants to make money from colony
   3. Quakers believe Holy Spirit (Inner Light) can inspire every man and woman, give women more equality than most Englishmen, refuse to bear arms
   4. Quakers much persecuted in England
   5. 1682, Penn arrives in America; founds capital of colony, Philadelphia; in next five years 8,000 Quakers arrive; Pennsylvania's toleration attracts other religious dissenters including Baptists, German sectarians, Presbyterians
   6. Coming as families, Quakers have rapid population growth through natural increase
   7. Penn drafts Frame of Government, creating governor, governor's council, legislature
   8. Pennsylvania has good relations with Native Americans because Penn buys land and deals fairly
   9. Pennsylvania prospers by growing grain and selling to West Indies; by 1700 Philadelphia a major port
   10. 1704, counties along lower Delaware River break away to form separate colony of Delaware
   11. Penn and the legislature often at odds; legislature resists proprietor's attempts to profit through rents and trade
   12. Middle colonies (New York, New Jersey, Pennsylvania, and Delaware) demonstrate benefits of pluralism: New York and New Jersey able to integrate Dutch and Swedes;

Pennsylvania, New Jersey, and Delaware impose no established church

V. **Rivals for North America**
   A. *France Claims a Continent*
      1. Louis XIV (1661–1715) turns New France into royal colony; 1660s, encourages French migration, sends French troops to defeat Native Americans blocking New France's expansion into Ohio Valley; after 1763, few French arrive, natural increase among settlers produces slow population growth
      2. Many French settlers become *coureurs de bois* (independent fur traders, living and intermarrying with Native Americans)
      3. *Coureurs* spread French empire over Ohio Valley, from Canada to mouth of Mississippi River; France tries to prevent Spain from linking Florida and New Mexico by consolidating New France in North American heartland
   B. *The Spanish Borderlands*
      1. 1716, first Spanish settlement in Texas
      2. 1680, Popé leads Pueblo Indian revolt against Spanish in New Mexico; many settlers flee to Mexico, leaving their horses behind; this is how Plains Indians first obtain horses
      3. Spanish recapture Taos twelve years later and reestablish their hold on New Mexico
      4. Spanish also face Native American rebellions in Florida; after 1715, Spanish reach agreement with Native Americans and offer freedom to English-owned slaves fleeing there
      5. Spain not in strong position to defend its far-flung but fragile empire in North America

Vocabulary

The following terms are used in Chapter 3. To understand the chapter fully, it is important that you know what each of them means.

yeoman in England, a small, landowning, independent farmer

tithes taxes due for the support of the clergy and church, usually one-tenth of one's income

established church a church officially recognized and given legal and financial support by the government

dissent to object or disagree

heresy an opinion or doctrine at variance with established religious beliefs

subversive tending to undermine existing or established institutions or doctrines; tending to cause the overthrow of existing governments or other established institutions

bicameral composed of two houses, chambers, or branches, as in a two-house legislative body

sacrament any of seven rites that the historical Christian church considered to have been instituted by Jesus to convey divine grace. Includes matrimony in Catholicism, but not in Puritan doctrine.

Identifications

After reading Chapter 3, you should be able to identify and explain the historical significance of each of the following:

John Winthrop and "A Model of Christian Charity"

conversion relation or sanctification

Old Deluder (Satan) Act

Roger Williams

Anne Hutchinson and the Antinomians

New England town meeting

Stuart Restoration

Pequot War

Metecom (King Philip's War)

"praying towns"

First Families of Virginia

Cecilius Calvert (Lord Baltimore)

Maryland Act for Religious Toleration

indentured servants

Anthony Ashley Cooper and John Locke

patroons

Peter Stuyvesant

William Penn and Penn's Frame of Government

coureurs de bois

Popé and the Pueblo Revolt (1680)

Skill Building: Maps

1. On the map of eastern North America and the Caribbean, locate each of the following and explain how its climate, soil, and other physical characteristics helped to shape the economy and society of the English colony or other European colony there.

    Massachusetts

    Rhode Island

    Connecticut

    North Carolina

    South Carolina

New York

New Jersey

Pennsylvania

Jamaica

the Bahamas

Barbados

Virginia

Maryland

2. On the map of North America, locate each of the following and explain its significance in seventeenth-century U.S. history.

lands claimed by France

Mississippi River

Ohio River

Gulf of Mexico

lands claimed by England

lands claimed by Spain

Texas

New Mexico

Florida

Great Lakes

34   *Chapter 3*

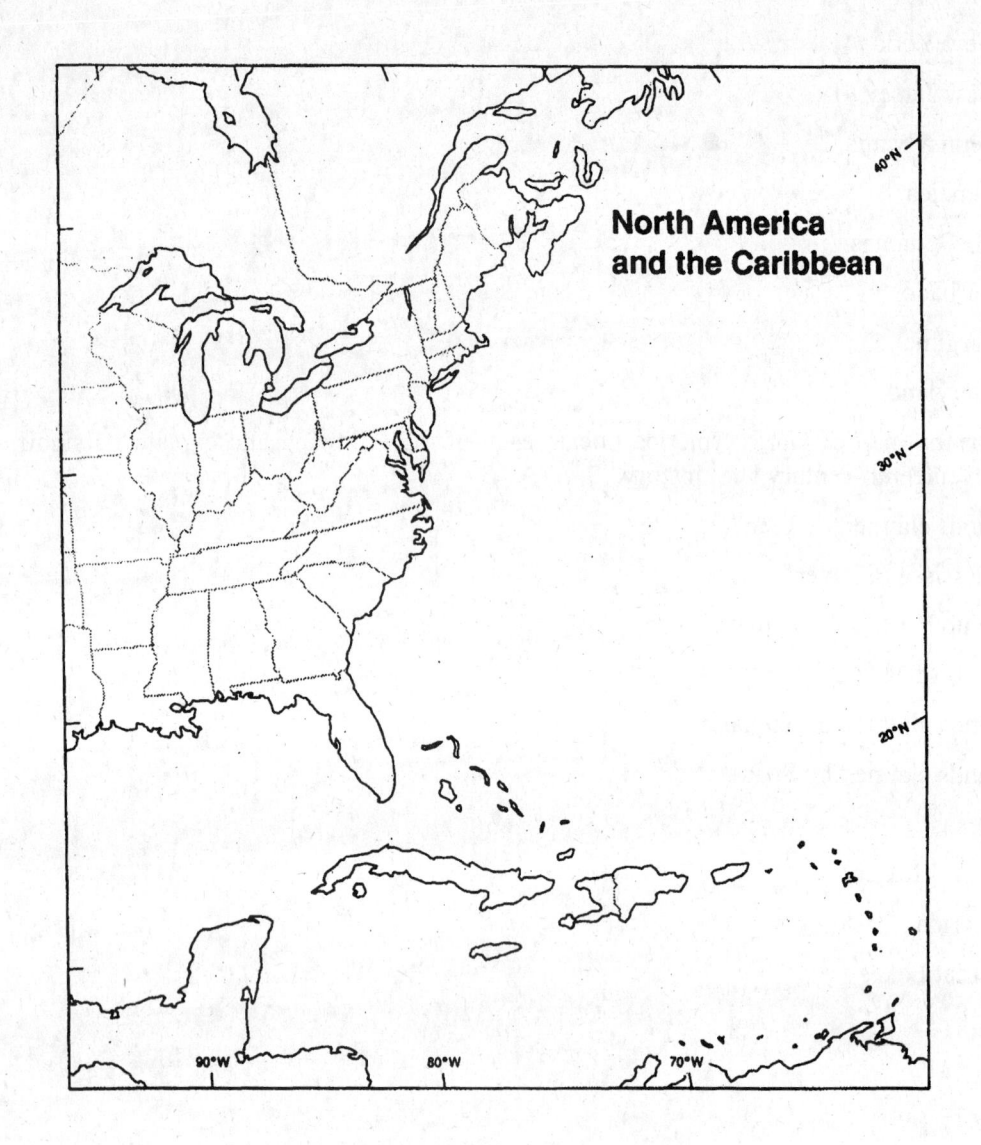

North America and the Caribbean

Expansion and Diversity: The Rise of Colonial America 35

North America

Multiple-Choice Questions

Circle the letter of the item that best completes each statement or answers the question.

1. The area with the longest life expectancy and the fastest population growth through natural increase in the seventeenth century was
   a. England.
   b. New England.
   c. the Chesapeake colonies.
   d. the British West Indies.

2. The first colony in English America that had separation of church and state and practiced religious tolerance was
   a. Maryland.
   b. Massachusetts.
   c. Rhode Island.
   d. Virginia.

3. Harvard College was chartered in 1636 primarily to
   a. train learned Puritan ministers.
   b. produce an educated governing class.
   c. educate lawyers who could defend the colonists' rights.
   d. teach Puritans how to farm the rocky New England soil.

4. A man's right to vote for governor and members of the General Court in seventeenth-century Massachusetts was based on
   a. landownership.
   b. wealth.
   c. length of residence in America.
   d. church membership.

5. The greatest extremes of inequality in landownership in the seventeenth century were found in
   a. New England.
   b. Maryland.
   c. the West Indies.
   d. Virginia.

6. The Half-Way Covenant was adopted because
   a. too few second- and third-generation Puritans were willing to testify publicly about their conversion experiences.
   b. Puritans believed that Native Americans were not capable of becoming fully Christian.
   c. Puritans wanted to justify enslavement of converted Native Americans and Africans.
   d. Puritans wanted to show Anglicans that they were willing to meet them halfway on resolving differences over religious doctrine.

7. By the late 1600s, which part of the British colonial empire had become an overwhelmingly black and slave society?
   a. New England
   b. Maryland
   c. Virginia
   d. the West Indies

8. Which of the following statements about Maryland is correct?
   a. It was founded by a joint-stock company.
   b. Although it was intended as a haven for Catholics, they were outnumbered by Protestant settlers, who passed anti-Catholic measures.
   c. The dominant crop that shaped its economy and society was sugar cane.
   d. Unlike neighboring Virginia, Maryland never adopted the institution of African slavery.

9. By the mid-1600s, which part of England's colonial empire was most ethnically and religiously diverse in population?
   a. New England
   b. Virginia and Maryland
   c. Carolinas
   d. the Middle Colonies

10. Which of the following statements about Virginia is correct?
    a. Unlike Massachusetts, it had no established church.
    b. It was governed by an appointed royal governor and Governor's Council and a House of Burgesses elected by landowners.
    c. By 1640 the great majority of its plantation laborers were African slaves.
    d. The indentured servants' chances of upward social mobility improved in the second half of the 1600s.

11. Which of the following statements about Pennsylvania is correct?
    a. William Penn allowed only Quakers to settle there.
    b. In the 1600s almost constant warfare occurred between the Quakers and the Native Americans in the area.
    c. William Penn grew rich from the monopoly he held on Pennsylvania's foreign trade and the rents he collected from his tenants.
    d. It did not have an established church and treated religious dissenters with tolerance.

12. King Philip's War
    a. was provoked by the unauthorized attacks on the Native Americans of Nathaniel Bacon and his followers.
    b. represented one of the few successful efforts of Native Americans to keep the English from encroaching on their lands.
    c. resulted in the slaughter or enslavement of many New England Native Americans and ended further resistance to white expansion.
    d. resulted in heavy loss of white lives in the Chesapeake area, contributing to the region's high mortality rates and slow population growth.

Essay Questions

1. "During the seventeenth century, New England evolved from a religious, community-oriented society to a region of rising worldliness, individualism, and competitiveness." Discuss how and why this evolution took place.

2. By 1715, the English mainland colonies had developed three distinct regional economies and societies: New England, Middle Colonies, and Southern Colonies. Compare and contrast the economies, social structures, and racial and ethnic compositions of these three regions.

3. Describe the extent of the British, French, and Spanish North American empires in 1700 and how they differed from each other in settlement and economic patterns. Discuss the relations each empire had with the Native Americans.

4. Discuss the ways in which the British West Indian colonies were intertwined with and affected the British mainland settlements.

5. Discuss the Salem witchcraft trials in Massachusetts and Bacon's Rebellion in Virginia. What does each incident reveal about the internal tensions and divisions within its respective colony?

Answers to Multiple-Choice Questions

1a. No. Poverty, landlessness, and disease took a heavy toll.
1b. Yes. Nearly even sex ratios and cold New England winters, which inhibited spread of contagious disease, made for rapid population growth. See page 40.
1c. No. Heavy preponderance of males in the area in first half of the seventeenth century and diseases slowed population growth.
1d. No. See 1c.

2a. No. 1654, Protestant majority repealed Act of Religious Toleration and barred Catholics from voting.
2b. No. Puritan faith was established church; dissenters were driven out.
2c. Yes. Under the influence of Roger Williams, no church was established and all religions were permitted. See page 38.
2d. No. The Church of England was established and tax monies were used to support it.

3a. Yes. Puritans believed that the faithful must be guided by highly educated clergymen. See page 37.
3b. No. It did produce an educated governing class, but that was not the main reason it was chartered.
3c. No. It did in time educate lawyers, but that was not the main reason it was chartered.
3d. No. Harvard in its early years gave a classical, not a practical, education.

4a. No. That was the rule in Virginia and some other colonies.
4b. No. Not the deciding factor.
4c. No. That was not the criteria in any American colony.
4d. Yes. See page 37.

5a. No. For religious reasons the Puritans tried to keep land holdings small and clustered around compact villages.
5b. No. By the late 1600 there were considerable inequalities, but not as great as in West Indies.
5c. Yes. See page 49.
5d. No. See 5b.

Expansion and Diversity: The Rise of Colonial America

6a. Yes. See page 41.
6b. No. The Half-Way Covenant had nothing to do with Native Americans.
6c. No. The Half-Way Covenant had nothing to do with slavery.
6d. No. Puritans still hoped to convince Anglicans that Puritan doctrine was what God approved of.

7a. No. The free white population of New England far exceeded the black, enslaved population.
7b. No. While the number of black slaves in Maryland increased considerably by the late 1600s, the white population was always in the majority.
7c. No. The same thing is true of Virginia as of Maryland.
7d. Yes. See page 49.

8a. No. It was a proprietary colony.
8b. Yes. See page 46.
8c. No. The dominant crop was tobacco.
8d. No. Maryland did adopt the institution of African slavery.

9a. No. New England had the most homogeneous population.
9b. No. Virginia and Maryland were predominantly of English extraction and Anglican.
9c. No. Carolinas were similar to Virginia and Maryland.
9d. Yes. See page 52.

10a. No. The established church in Virginia was Anglican.
10b. Yes. See page 45.
10c. No. Until about 1700 the majority of plantation laborers in Virginia were white indentured servants.
10d. No. They worsened.

11a. No. Penn opened Pennsylvania to all who wished to come.
11b. No. Because Penn dealt fairly with the Native Americans, there was relatively little conflict.
11c. No. Because Penn found it almost impossible to collect rents and control trade.
11d. Yes. See page 53–54.

12a. No. Bacon's rebellion occurred in Virginia.
12b. No. The Indians were crushed in King Philip's War.
12c. Yes. See page 42.
12d. No. King Philip's War took place in New England.

Copyright © Houghton Mifflin Company. All rights reserved.

CHAPTER 4
The Bonds of Empire, 1660–1750

Outline

I. **Rebellion and War**

   A. *Royal Centralization*
   1. Last Stuart kings, Charles II and James II, dislike representative government; try to rule without Parliament in England and colonial assemblies in America
   2. New England resists; Massachusetts defies Navigation Acts
   3. Charles II punishes Massachusetts: 1679, takes some of its territory to form New Hampshire; 1684, revokes Massachusetts charter, makes it royal colony
   4. James II even more arbitrary; 1686–1688, merges all New England colonies, plus New York and New Jersey, into Dominion of New England; abolishes their assemblies, puts full power in hands of dictatorial governor, Sir Edmond Andros
   5. Colonists bitterly resent denial of their rights; tensions high in Massachusetts and New York

   B. *The Glorious Revolution in England and America*
   1. 1688, James II's high-handed and pro-Catholic actions lead to Glorious Revolution; James flees; William and Mary take throne and agree to limited monarchy as defined in English Bill of Rights (1689)
   2. 1689, Massachusetts, New York, Maryland rebel against Stuart-appointed governors; uprisings reestablish representative government, ensure Protestant religious freedom
   3. Dominion of New England dissolved; charters and colonial assemblies restored; Massachusetts's new royal charter (1691) does not allow as much Puritan domination and self-rule as formerly; monarch appoints governor; property ownership, not Puritan church membership, becomes requirement for vote
   4. 1689–1691, Jacob Leisler and followers rule New York; 1691, Leisler executed for refusing to turn over authority to newly arrived English troops
   5. 1689–1692, John Coode leads Protestant rebellion in Maryland; Church of England becomes established church

   C. *A Generation of War*
   1. 1689, England and its allies fight France in War of League of Augsburg (King William's War in America)

2. 1702, Queen Anne's War; French and Native Americans from Canada attack New England towns; Spanish attack South Carolina; war ends with French and Native Americans still in control of the interior
3. Wars unify Anglo-Americans, make them aware of their need for English protection, make them more loyal to Crown

II. Colonial Economies and Societies
   A. *Mercantilist Empires in America*
   1. Policies followed by Britain, France, and Spain toward their colonies in America guided by mercantilism
   2. Mercantilist theory says nation should increase its wealth in gold and silver by producing as much as possible of its own needs within its empire; export to foreign competitors more than you buy from them
   3. British Parliament, starting in 1651, passes Navigation Acts to implement mercantilist theory
   4. Navigation Acts require all trade to be conducted on British-owned ships; bar Americans from selling certain products: tobacco, rice, furs, indigo, naval stores, to foreign countries unless they first pass through England; place high taxes on products Americans buy outside of empire, like molasses from French Caribbean
   5. Though the laws cut into profits of tobacco and rice planters a bit, they do not much hurt colonists because they smuggle in goods and Navigation Acts also benefit American economy
   6. Navigation Acts stimulate growth of American merchant marine, shipbuilding, ports; bounties paid to producers of hemp, lumber, and other items encourages development of those industries in colonies
   7. British colonies develop robust economies; French and Spanish empires do not flourish under mercantilism
   8. Main export of French colonies, fur, does not bring in profit; French government loses money in trade with Indians, aimed at cementing good relations with Native American allies
   9. Spain does little manufacturing but insists her colonies buy finished goods only from her; this drives Spanish colonists into widespread smuggling of British and French products
   10. Though all three mother countries follow mercantilist policies, mercantilism does not work well for France and Spain because they lack large merchant class with liquid assets to invest in their colonies and other commercial ventures that the British have

   B. *A Burgeoning, Diversifying Population*
   1. French and Spanish colonies in North America lag behind British in population growth as well as economic development
   2. 1750, British North America has 1,700,000 non-Indian inhabitants; New France, 60,000; Spanish North America, 19,000
   3. After 1700, British North American population grows rapidly from natural increase and immigration

4. Eighteenth-century immigrants come less from England, more from other places: 140,000 West Africans brought on slave ships under horrible conditions; 100,000 Irish and Scots-Irish, 65,000 Germans arrive
5. English colonies becoming more racially and ethnically diverse, sometimes resented by colonists of English extraction
6. Eighteenth-century immigrants tend to push into piedmont region, where land is cheaper; 1750, one-third of colonial population reside there
7. After 1713, importation of slaves to North America greatly increases; 1750, blacks 20 percent of North American colonists; most live in South; 15 percent live north of Maryland; black and white populations both grow through natural increase

C. Rural Men and Women
1. Most rural families work small farms; children do not inherit much land
2. Most couples rent land until they reach mid-thirties; must borrow money to buy land; not out of debt until their fifties
3. Wives and daughters supplement family income with home manufacturing

D. Colonial Farmers and the Environment
1. Eighteenth-century farmers cut down forests to bring more land under cultivation; use timber for fences, fuel, buildings; sell wood to townspeople
2. Deforestation drives away large game; causes greater extremes in temperature and less dependable water level in streams; amount of fish declines
3. Farmers grow tobacco and other soil-depleting crops without fertilizer or crop rotation; as result, land loses fertility and yields diminish

E. The Urban Paradox
1. After 1740, 4 percent of colonists live in cities; have less economic mobility than rural Americans
2. Colonial cities plagued by poverty, crowding, poor sanitation, epidemics, periodic recessions; result, urban residents have life span 10 years shorter than rural residents

F. Slavery's Wages
1. 1750s, blacks comprise 20 percent of New York City population and majority of Charles Town and Savannah
2. Slaves work harder and longer for less reward than white indentured servants
3. As black percentage of population increases, whites impose harsher controls; slaves respond with violence as in 1739 Stono Rebellion in South Carolina and 1712 and 1741 incidents in New York City; whites suppress with brutality and greater repression

G. The Rise of the Colonial Elites
1. For colonial whites, status defined by wealth
2. After 1720 outward shows of wealth more obvious
3. Wealthy attempt to imitate fashions and life-styles of European upper class
4. Gap between wealthy and poor in eighteenth-century colonial cities great, but not as pronounced as in European cities

H. *Elites and Colonial Politics*
   1. Elites dominate colonial politics and society
   2. Elites appointed to governor's councils and judgeships; elected to colonial assemblies
   3. Women, blacks, Native Americans cannot vote; property qualifications exclude about 40 percent of white males from voting; voter turnout in rural areas low
   4. After 1700 power shifts away from royal governors to elected assemblies; colonial assemblies influence governors by controlling their salaries
   5. Assemblies authorize spending and impose taxes; Board of Trade ineffective in enforcing royal authority
   6. Colonies become increasingly self-governing, except for setting trade regulations, printing money, declaring war

III. Competing for a Continent
   A. *France and Native Americans*
      1. After end of War of Spanish Succession (1713), France resumes empire building in North America
      2. 1718, French found New Orleans
      3. Settlers survive by combination of farming, hunting, fishing and, above all, trading with Native Americans
      4. French also expand their trade and relations with Native Americans in Ohio Valley and on Great Plains; trade goods and horses that Indians acquire from Europeans allow Sioux and other Plains tribes to develop nomadic way of life based on hunting buffalo
      5. French generally more successful than British in getting along with Native Americans; French also crush tribes that stand in their way, such as Natchez
   B. *Native Americans and British Expansion*
      1. British colonies, too, expanding at expense of Native Americans
      2. Pennsylvania forces Delaware Indians to cede their lands and move close to Iroquois
      3. Other Eastern tribes also pushed westward and are used by Iroquois as buffer between themselves and aggressive English
   C. *British Expansion in the South: Georgia*
      1. 1732, Parliament charters colony of Georgia and gives some tax support for its founding
      2. James Oglethorpe, its early leader, wants Georgia to be haven for English debtors and buffer against Spanish in Florida
      3. 1733, Oglethorpe establishes Savannah; 1740, about 3,000 in Georgia, but majority not debtors; almost one-half other Europeans, not English
      4. Oglethorpe's ban on slavery and restrictions on size of landholdings discourage immigrants

5. 1750, ban on slavery lifted; land restrictions also end; Georgia becomes prosperous growing rice on big plantations; 1770, Georgia population 23,000, almost one-half are black slaves

D. *Spain's Struggles*
1. To fend off Native Americans, French, and British, Spain spreads its empire throughout Southwest
2. Spain grants vast land holdings for *ranchos* in New Mexico; 5,200 Spanish settlers and 13,500 Pueblo Indians live in New Mexico by 1750
3. Spain establishes four missions in Texas, including Alamo, but only 1,200 Spanish go to live in Texas
4. 1750, Spain controls Southeast and Southwest; France, the Mississippi, Ohio, and Missouri River Valleys; European population of New Spain and New France small and dependent on Native American goodwill; British Atlantic coastal colonies, compact, more European population, aggressively expansionist toward Native Americans

IV. Enlightenment and Awakening

A. *Introduction*
1. Eighteenth-century Anglo-Americans have highest literacy rate in world; New England white males highest rate in America
2. Ordinary Americans live in world of oral culture; elites in world of print culture, well acquainted with ideas of European Enlightenment

B. *The Enlightenment in America*
1. American intellectuals inspired by Enlightenment ideals: belief in reason, science, natural law; impressed by work of Sir Isaac Newton and John Locke
2. Benjamin Franklin embodies Enlightenment ideals: publisher of *Poor Richard's Almanack,* scientific experimenter and inventor, organizer of American Philosophical Society
3. Franklin, Thomas Jefferson, and many other Enlightenment intellectuals become Deists, believing that God created the universe to operate according to natural laws

C. *The Great Awakening*
1. Religious revival, the Great Awakening, sweeps through Anglo-America in 1740s
2. Preachers of Great Awakening (Jonathan Edwards, George Whitefield, others) stress corrupt human nature, divine fury, need for immediate repentance and conversion
3. Emotionalism and attacks of radical preachers on established clergy lead to split between New Lights and Old Lights
4. Great Awakening splits American Protestantism into many more denominations, stimulates founding of new colleges, converts large numbers of African-Americans and Native Americans to Protestantism, encourages religious tolerance and questioning of established authority (civil and religious), increases importance of women in colonial religion

Vocabulary

The following terms are used in Chapter 4. To understand the chapter fully, it is important that you know what each of them means.

provincialism displaying a narrow or localized outlook or life-style; displaying a countrified or rustic outlook or life-style

coup sudden overthrow of a government

urbanization the growth of cities

autonomy self-government, independence

dowry the money, goods, or estate that a woman brings to her husband at marriage

paradox situation that seems contrary to common sense yet is the case

artisans persons skilled in industrial arts or crafts—for example, silversmiths and blacksmiths

journeyman person who has learned a skilled trade and works at it for another person

deferential yielding to the opinions or wishes of another

oral culture way of life in which people normally obtain most of their information and communicate by word of mouth

print culture way of life in which people rely on books, newspapers, and other printed sources for much of their information

Identifications

After reading Chapter 4, you should be able to identify and explain the historical significance of each of the following:

Sir Edmond Andros and the Dominion of New England

Glorious Revolution and English Bill of Rights, 1689

Leisler's Rebellion

John Coode

King William's War and Queen Anne's War

redemptioners

mercantilism and the Navigation Acts

Adam Smith, *The Wealth of Nations*

Stono Rebellion

Board of Trade

James Oglethorpe

Enlightenment

Benjamin Franklin

Deists

Great Awakening
Jonathan Edwards
George Whitefield
New Lights versus Old Lights

Skill Building: Maps

1. On the map of eastern North America, label each of the thirteen British mainland colonies that existed in 1750. Locate each of the major port cities of Anglo-America in the eighteenth century: Savannah, Charles Town, Philadelphia, New York, and Boston. Locate the Hudson River, the tidewater and piedmont regions, and the Appalachians. What was the historical importance of each of these in eighteenth-century Anglo-America? Indicate the areas in which each of the following was mainly grown: rice, tobacco, wheat, and corn. Explain the economic and social impact on life in the area where each was the chief crop.

2. On the map of North America, locate each of the following and explain its significance in eighteenth-century American history:

   lands claimed by France

   Mississippi River

   Arkansas River

   Ohio River

   Gulf of Mexico

   New Orleans

   lands claimed by Spain

   San Antonio

   Santa Fe

   Florida

   Great Lakes

The Bonds of Empire, 1660–1750

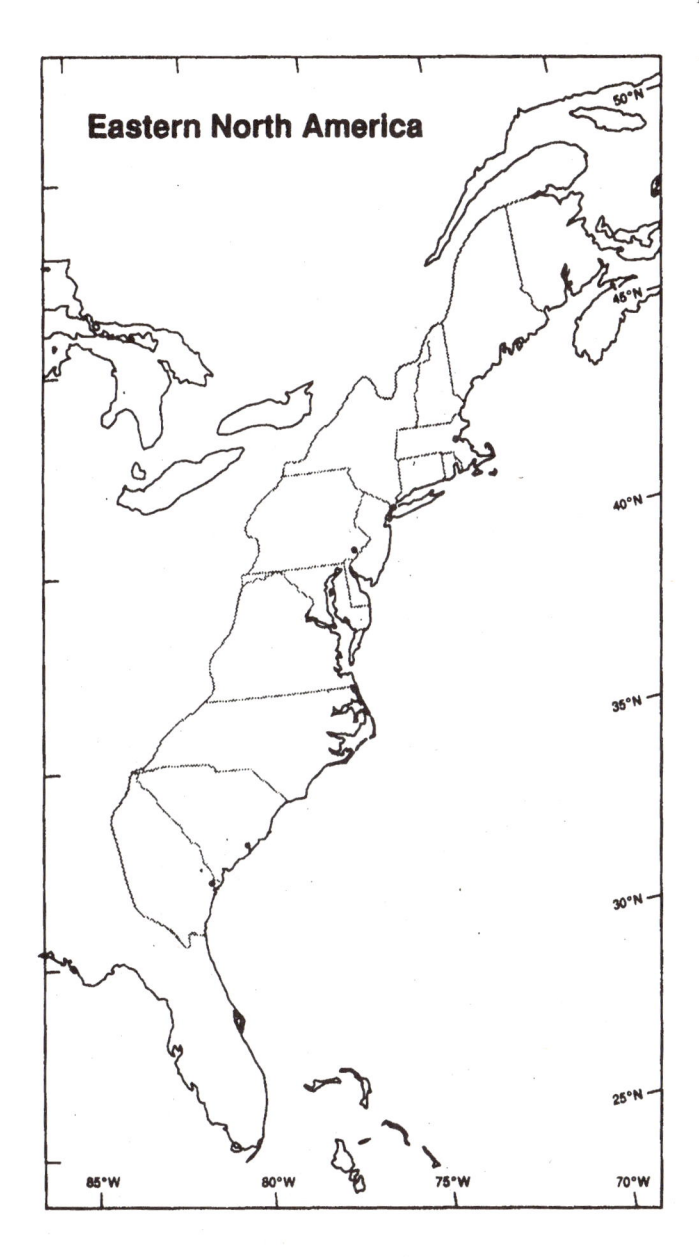

Eastern North America

48 *Chapter 4*

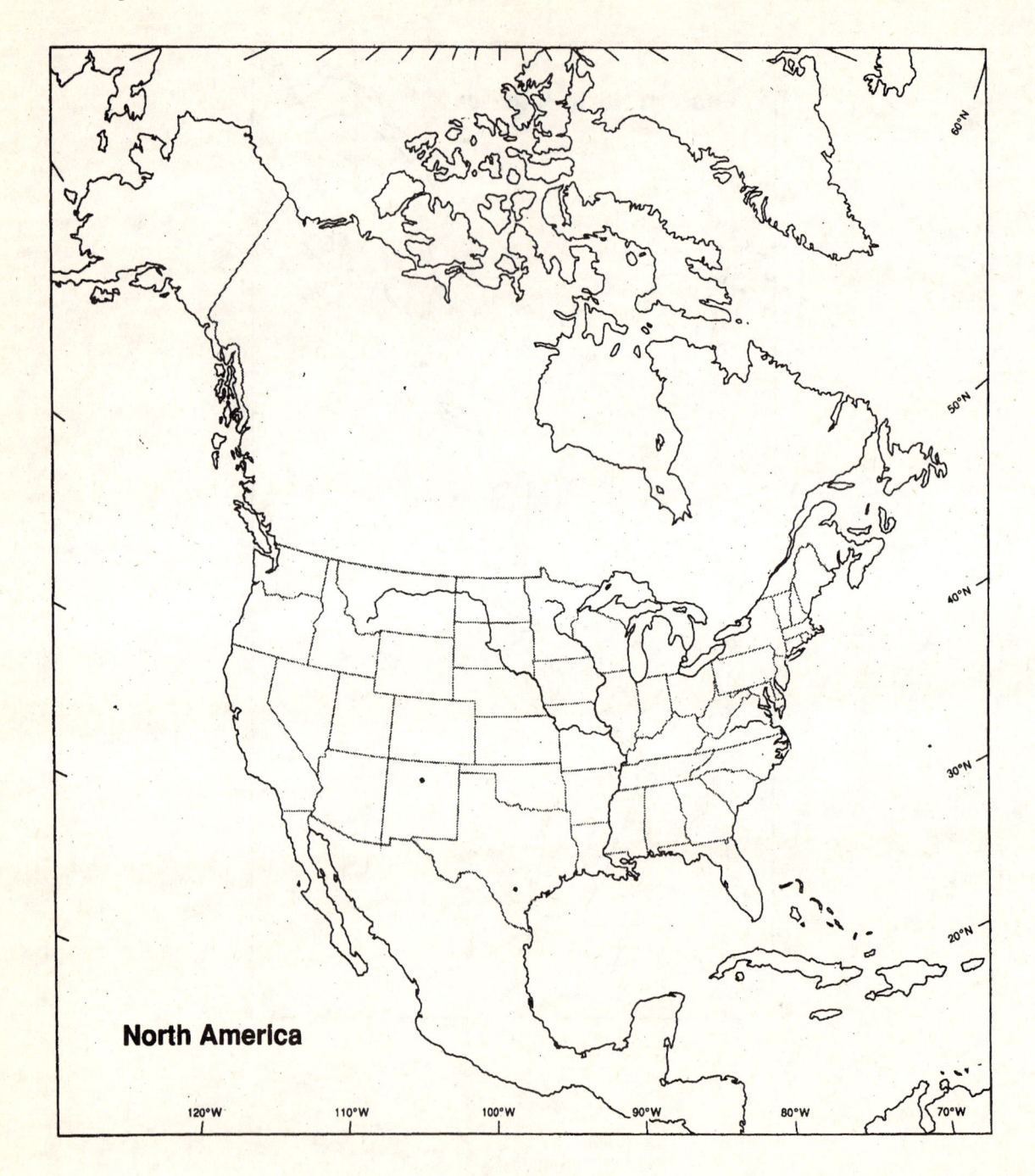

North America

Multiple-Choice Questions

Circle the letter of the item that best completes each statement or answers the question.

1. Which of the following statements about the Anglo-American colonies in 1750 is correct?
   a. Colonists living in the port cities were much more prosperous than those in the countryside.
   b. Many new colleges were established between the 1740s and 1770s.
   c. Most immigrants to the colonies were from England; fewer came from other parts of Europe.
   d. The overall standard of living had risen little since 1700.

2. Which of the following statements about blacks and slavery in Anglo-America in the 1700s is correct?
   a. As more Europeans settled in the 1700s, the percentage of blacks in Anglo-America declined.
   b. White indentured servants were worked harder and treated more harshly than black slaves because masters had no property owners' interest in the indentured servants.
   c. Racial tensions in colonial cities heightened as the percentage of black slaves living in them rose significantly.
   d. Because black slaves were generally peaceful, whites showed little apprehension about blacks and slavery.

3. Which of the following statements concerning colonial government between 1700 and 1763 is correct?
   a. The royal governors and the Board of Trade frequently vetoed or disallowed laws passed by the colonial legislatures.
   b. All white men had the right to vote and hold office.
   c. The lower house of a colonial legislature was generally dominated by representatives of the lower and middle classes, whereas the upper house was dominated by the wealthy.
   d. The colonial legislatures became a powerful force in American government, controlling taxes, the budget, and executive salaries.

4. James Oglethorpe
   a. hoped Georgia would be a home for English debtors and a barrier to Spanish expansion northward.
   b. encouraged the importation of African slaves to Georgia in order to promote profitable rice cultivation there.
   c. led the Stono Rebellion.
   d. all of the above

5. Which of the following statements about women in eighteenth-century America is correct?
   a. Women could not inherit their parents' land. Only sons could legally inherit family estates.
   b. Women could not choose their own husbands. The choice was made by their parents.
   c. Women in rural and urban families played an important part in helping to support their households.
   d. Women had legal control over their dowries and other property that they brought with them to marriage.

6. When the American colonists learned of the Glorious Revolution,
   a. they declared their independence from the mother country.
   b. those living in the southern colonies declared their continuing loyalty to the Stuart kings.
   c. those living in Maryland petitioned the new monarchs, William and Mary, to be allowed to keep Catholicism as the favored religion in their colony.
   d. those living in Massachusetts, New York, and Maryland rebelled against and drove out their Stuart-appointed governors.

7. Which of the following resulted from King William's and Queen Anne's wars?
   a. The French were driven from the North American continent.
   b. The Stuart kings were driven from power.
   c. The wars heightened Anglo-Americans' sense of their English identity and make them feel dependent on the mother country for protection.
   d. The English captured New Orleans and started to settle Louisiana.

8. The Dominion of New England was
   a. created by James II to consolidate his hold on the northern colonies and eliminate their colonial assemblies.
   b. welcomed by most New Englanders because it broke the Massachusetts Puritans' dictatorial rule over the region.
   c. continued by William and Mary because the administrative consolidation made it easier to enforce the Navigation Acts.
   d. created as part of the reforms instituted after the Glorious Revolution.

9. The highest literacy rate in the eighteenth century was found in
   a. England.
   b. New England.
   c. the middle colonies, from New York to Delaware.
   d. Virginia and the Carolinas.

10. Which of these institutions of higher learning was *not* founded during the time of the Great Awakening?
    a. Harvard
    b. Princeton
    c. Rutgers
    d. Columbia

11. Which of the following was a slave uprising that badly frightened white society?
    a. Leisler's Rebellion
    b. Coode's Rebellion
    c. Stono Rebellion
    d. Popé's revolt

12. In the 1700s the colonial empire in North America with the highest standard of living and the fastest growing economy was that of
    a. Spain.
    b. Britain.
    c. France.
    d. Holland.

Essay Questions

1. How much equality, liberty, and self-government existed in the American colonies in the period 1700–1750? Back up your assessment with as many specific facts as possible.

2. What was the Great Awakening? Who was attracted to it? Who was repelled by it? What impact did it have on religious, social, educational, and political developments in eighteenth-century America?

3. Discuss the racial and ethnic makeup and the social class structure of mid-eighteenth-century America.

4. Historians have long debated the impact of Britain's mercantilist economic policy on the colonies. Explain the mercantilist economic theory and show how Parliament incorporated it into the navigation system. According to Chapter 4, in what ways did the system hurt and benefit America? Does the author believe that the harm outweighed the benefits?

5. In the second quarter of the eighteenth century, "no American more fully embodied the Enlightenment spirit than Benjamin Franklin." Discuss Franklin's life, beliefs, career, and achievements, and explain how they embodied the Enlightenment spirit.

Answers to Multiple-Choice Questions

1a. No. There was growing poverty in colonial port cities in the 1700s.
1b. Yes. These included Princeton, Columbia, Brown, Rutgers, and Dartmouth.
1c. No. In the 1700s many non-English settled in the British colonies.
1d. No. Overall standard of living rose markedly.

2a. No. The percentage of blacks rose because of heavy slave importation in the 1700s.
2b. No. Slaves worked harder and longer and were given less sustenance than white indentured servants.
2c. Yes. This was especially true in cities where the slave population became the majority, as in Charles Town. See page 68.
2d. No. Slave resistance, such as the Stono Rebellion in South Carolina and the 1712 and 1741 troubles in New York City, made whites apprehensive, vengeful, and brutal.

Copyright © Houghton Mifflin Company. All rights reserved.

3a. No. They usually did not because governors feared colonial assemblies would cut their salaries, and the Board of Trade did not pay close attention to the American colonies.
3b. No. Property requirements disqualified about 40 percent of white males from voting, and the expense of holding office kept all but the wealthy from serving.
3c. No. Both houses were dominated by the wealthy.
3d. Yes. See page 72.

4a. Yes. See page 74.
4b. No. Oglethrope banned slavery in Georgia until he was forced to give in to the settlers' demands for it in 1750.
4c. No. This was a slave rebellion in South Carolina.
4d. No. See 4b and 4c.

5a. No. Both sons and daughters could inherit in most colonies.
5b. No. Women could choose their own mates.
5c. Yes. See pages 66–67.
5d. No. The husband gained legal control over the dowry and any other property the wife brought into the marriage.

6a. No. They were a long way from thoughts of independence in the late 1600s.
6b. No. There was little support for the Stuart kings in the American colonies.
6c. No. The majority in Maryland were Protestants who had already passed discriminatory laws against Catholics.
6d. Yes. Rebellions in 1689 in all three colonies drove out the Sutart-appointed governors. See pages 61–62.

7a. No. French settlement continued to expand.
7b. No. That happened as a result of the Glorious Revolution, which took place prior to those two wars.
7c. Yes. See page 62.
7d. No. New Orleans stayed in French hands.

8a. Yes. See page 60.
8b. No. Most New Englanders hated the Dominion of New England and its dictatorial governor, Sir Edmond Andros, who closed their legislatures and threatened all of their other liberties.
8c. No. William and Mary returned charters to the New England colonies and allowed them to reestablish their assemblies.
8d. No. It was created by James II to consolidate his power over New England and get rid of colonial assemblies.

9a. No. Only about 30 percent of the English population was literate.
9b. Yes. 90 percent of the white men and 40 percent of the white women were literate.
9c. No. The literacy rate in those colonies was between 35 and 50 percent.
9d. No. See 9c.

10a. Yes. It was founded in 1636, over a century before the Great Awakening.
10b. No. It was founded in the period 1740s through 1760s, the time of the Great Awakening.
10c. No. See 10b.
10d. No. See 10b.

11a. No. This was an uprising of New York colonists against Stuart-appointed officials.
11b. No. This was an uprising of Maryland colonists against the Stuart-appointed governor.
11c. Yes. This was a slave rebellion in South Carolina in 1739.
11d. No. This was an Indian revolt against the Spanish in New Mexico.

12a. No. Spain's North American colonies were poor, struggling outposts.
12b. Yes. See page 78.
12c. No. Like Spain, France's North American colonies were poor, struggling outposts.
12d. No. By the 1700s Holland had no colonies left in North America.

CHAPTER 5
Roads to Revolution, 1744–1776

Outline

I. Imperial Warfare

   A. *King George's War*
 1. 1745, New Englanders capture Louisbourg in Nova Scotia from French
 2. In 1748 treaty, Great Britain returns Louisbourg to France, provoking colonial resentment

   B. *A Fragile Peace*
 1. 1752, Virginia, Pennsylvania, France, Iroquois, other Native Americans all claim Ohio Valley
 2. 1753, France starts building chain of forts in Ohio Valley
 3. George Washington tries to block French, but is driven out of Ohio Valley
 4. 1754, seven northern colonies attempt to band together for defense in Albany Plan of Union; plan fails because colonial assemblies will not turn over power; Albany Plan sets precedent for future union

   C. *The Seven Years' War in America*
 1. 1755, war breaks out in America between French and British; 1756, Seven Years' War starts in Europe
 2. At first, war goes badly for Anglo-Americans; 1758, turning point
 3. Native American allies desert French; Prime Minister William Pitt offers financial support for colonials if they will assume most of the fighting in America
 4. Colonials flock to the struggle, help British take Louisbourg and Fort Duquesne (1758), Quebec (1759), Montreal (1760); French resistance crumbles
 5. In Treaty of Paris (1763) French cede all territories on North American mainland to either British or Spanish; size of British empire quadruples
 6. British expel Acadians from Canada; most flee to Louisiana, where they are called Cajuns
 7. These wars strengthen bonds between British and her colonies, but also plant seeds of future conflict

II. Imperial Reorganization

   A. *Introduction*
1. After Seven Years' War, Great Britain tries to tighten control over its expanded colonial empire and finance its administration with new taxes on Englishmen at home and overseas
2. These efforts arouse opposition in colonies on economic and constitutional grounds

   B. *Friction among Allies*
1. Friction builds between British and Anglo-Americans after French defeat
2. Reasons for friction: Anglo-Americans feel British do not give them enough credit for the victory; British resent paying colonials for fighting to defend themselves; new conflicts with Native Americans in Ohio Valley (Neolin, Pontiac) force British to send more troops, spend more money, issue Proclamation of 1763 (slowing westward settlement); colonists resent proclamation, continuing presence of British troops, and British demands that they pay taxes to mother country

   C. *The Writs of Assistance*
1. To stop smuggling, British use writs of assistance (general search warrants that permit officials to enter any ship or building to search for and seize smuggled goods)
2. 1761, James Otis argues before Massachusetts Supreme Court that writs of assistance unconstitutional; loses case
3. Still, Otis and most colonists believe Parliament does not have authority to violate their traditional rights as Englishmen

   D. *The Sugar Act*
1. 1764, Parliament adopts Sugar Act to raise revenue; import duties placed on sugar
2. Law violates right to fair trial; accused smugglers to be tried in vice-admiralty courts, without juries, by judges with financial stake in finding defendant guilty

   E. *The Stamp Act*
1. Prime Minister George Grenville and most British think colonists should contribute more tax money for upkeep of empire
2. 1765, Parliament passes Stamp Act; Americans must buy and use stamped paper for periodicals, wills, contracts, and other documents; violators to be tried in vice-admiralty courts
3. Stamp Act is internal tax; affects many more people than external tax such as Sugar Act
4. Grenville defends Stamp Act as legal because colonists have virtual representation in Parliament (each member of House of Commons represents interests of all of empire, not just those of his constituents)
5. Colonists reject virtual representation, believe in actual representation
6. Colonists accept right of Parliament to regulate trade of the empire but claim that only their assemblies can tax them to raise revenue

Roads to Revolution, 1744–1776   55

 F. *Resisting the Stamp Act*
  1. Virginia House of Burgesses adopts Patrick Henry's resolutions denying Parliament's right to tax the colonies; eight other provincial assemblies concur
  2. Boston artisans and businessmen found Loyal Nine to fight Stamp Act; similar groups, called Sons of Liberty, form in other cities
  3. Loyal Nine and Sons of Liberty direct mobs in attacks on stamp distributors; all resign their posts
  4. October 1765, representatives from nine colonies convene in Stamp Act Congress in New York; protest taxation without representation and denial of trial by jury
  5. Merchants organize boycott of British goods; British business community pleads with Parliament to repeal Stamp Act
  6. March 1766, Parliament revokes Stamp Act; passes Declaratory Act: Parliament has legislative power over colonies in all things, including imposing taxes
 G. *Ideology, Religion, and Resistance*
  1. Influenced by John Locke, by English oppositionist writers and radicals, and by ideas from classical Rome and Greece, educated colonists see in Parliament's actions a conspiracy of corrupt government to deny them natural rights
  2. Protestant clergymen, except Anglicans, preach that American resistance to British tyranny and corruption is blow against sin and for God

III. The Deepening Crisis
 A. *The Quartering Act*
  1. 1767, Charles Townshend, chancellor of exchequer, takes lead in making colonial policy
  2. Townshend shows his readiness to interfere with colonial self-government in his drafting of New York Suspending Act: all laws passed by assembly nullified if it will not vote money to supply British soldiers, required under Quartering Act
 B. *The Townshend Duties*
  1. Parliament passes Revenue Act of 1767 (Townshend duties): import taxes levied on glass, paint, lead, paper, tea
  2. Townshend wants to use money from duties to pay salaries of royal governors—to weaken colonial assemblies' financial hold over them
 C. *The Colonists' Reaction*
  1. 1767, John Dickinson's *Letters from a Farmer in Pennsylvania* states Parliament cannot impose revenue-raising duties on colonists who have no representation in that body
  2. 1768, Massachusetts assembly sends Samuel Adams's "circular letter," making the same point, to other colonial legislatures; Virginia and others concur
  3. 1768, Boston and other merchants boycott British imports
  4. Boycott cuts imports by about 40 percent
 D. *Wilkes and Liberty*

Copyright © Houghton Mifflin Company. All rights reserved.

1. British merchants and artisans hurt by colonial boycott, implore Parliament to repeal Townshend duties
2. Their appeal part of larger British protest movement against policies of George III and Parliament dominated by tiny elite of wealthy landowners
3. London journalist John Wilkes leads the unrest; British government arrests him, denies him seat in House of Commons to which he had been elected
4. Government's actions prompt dissident Englishmen and Americans to question further authority of an unrepresentative Parliament

E. Women and Colonial Resistance
1. Women bolster protest against Townshend duties
2. Women refuse to serve taxed tea; organize spinning bees to produce cloth and clothing at home, cutting imports from England

F. Customs Racketeering
1. 1767, Parliament creates American Board of Customs Commissioners to enforce Navigation Acts; increases number of port officials, funds Coast Guard patrols to catch smugglers, pays informers
2. Corrupt customs officials seize ships and cargoes, levy fines for technical violations of Navigation and Sugar Acts; break open sailors' chests to search for small amounts of undeclared merchandise
3. Seamen and others retaliate with violent attacks on paid informers and customs officials; 1768, *Liberty* incident in Boston
4. Actions of customs commissioners contribute to Americans' suspicions of British motives and alienation from mother country
5. Customs racketeering also makes Americans broaden their stand on Parliament from "no taxation without representation" to "no legislation at all without representation"

G. The Boston Massacre
1. 1768, British send more soldiers to Boston to quell violence
2. Samuel Adams's *Journal of the Times* fans Bostonian resentment
3. 1770, Boston Massacre: mob threatens Boston customs office; British soldiers open fire, killing five
4. British remove troops to fortified island in Boston harbor; promise to put soldiers who fired on trial
5. Patriot leader John Adams serves as soldiers' lawyer in interests of fair trial

H. Lord North's Partial Retreat
1. 1770, Lord North becomes prime minister; sponsors repeal all Townshend duties except one on tea
2. Americans resent Parliament's continuing claim to right to tax them; keep up tea boycott
3. Tea tax brings in too little money to pay governors' salaries

I. The Committees of Correspondence

Roads to Revolution, 1744–1776   57

        1. 1772, Lord North tries to go ahead with plan to pay royal governors from customs revenues
        2. Samuel Adams organizes committees of correspondence in Massachusetts to coordinate resistance; committees spring up in every colony but Pennsylvania, linking Americans in communications web
   J. Frontier Tensions
        1. British government unable to enforce Proclamation of 1763; land-hungry colonists press westward
        2. Westward expansion leads to violence against Native Americans, clashes between colonists: 1769 fight of New Hampshire Green Mountain Boys against New York landlords
        3. Western settlers fight with eastern-dominated colonial governments: Carolina Regulators, Battle of Alamance Creek, 1771

IV. Toward Independence
   A. *The Tea Act*
        1. 1773, British East India Company on verge of bankruptcy because of Americans' smuggling and nonconsumption of tea
        2. 1773, Parliament passes Tea Act to save company; allows company to sell directly to American consumers, cutting out middlemen; tea will cost less even with tax on it than smuggled tea
        3. Committees of correspondence denounce act as trick to sell taxed tea and to raise revenue to pay governors' salaries; committees organize to prevent landing of company's ships and sale of cargo
        4. December 1773, Samuel Adams addresses Boston protest meeting; members of audience board company's ships in harbor, throw tea overboard (Boston Tea Party)
   B. *The Coercive Acts*
        1. British retaliate for Boston Tea Party with Intolerable (Coercive) Acts: close Boston harbor, revoke Massachusetts charter and restructure its government to make it less democratic, requisition privately owned buildings to quarter troops, send authorities charged with killing colonials to England for trial
        2. General Thomas Gage, North American military commander, appointed Massachusetts governor
        3. These measures and unrelated Quebec Act (providing no elected legislature for that province) convince colonists that British intend to destroy representative government and civil liberties in America

Chapter 5

    C. The First Continental Congress
       1. 1774, to resist Intolerable Acts, all colonies but Georgia send delegates to Continental Congress in Philadelphia
       2. Congress approves Suffolk Resolves: colonies will not obey Intolerable Acts, Americans will defend themselves against British troops
       3. Congress creates Continental Association to enforce total cutoff of trade with England and British West Indies; petitions George III to dismiss ministers responsible for Intolerable Acts
    D. The Fighting Begins
       1. Committees of Continental Association coerce wavering colonists into cooperating with trade ban, intimidate loyalists (Tories)
       2. Volunteer militias (minutemen) take up arms and drill; extralegal congresses meet
       3. April 1775, General Gage sends 700 British soldiers to Lexington and Concord to seize weapons, arrest patriot leaders
       4. Minutemen fight troops at Lexington and Concord; besiege Boston; fight battles of Breed's and Bunker Hill; May 1775, Ethan Allen and Green Mountain Boys capture Fort Ticonderoga
       5. May 1775, Second Continental Congress meets, sends Olive Branch Petition to George III, seeking cease-fire at Boston, repeal of Intolerable Acts, negotiations about American rights
       6. King rejects petition; December 1775, Parliament declares colonies in rebellion
    E. The Failure of Reconciliation
       1. 1775, majority of Americans still hope for reconciliation
       2. Second Continental Congress establishes American continental army and appoints George Washington commander
       3. 1776, Thomas Paine's *Common Sense* turns Americans away from lingering loyalty to king, toward independence
    F. Declaring Independence
       1. June 1776, Virginia delegation proposes that Congress declare independence
       2. July 2, Congress adopts Virginia resolution and creates new nation
       3. Congress instructs Thomas Jefferson to draft declaration justifying separation from England
       4. Influenced by Enlightenment ideals, Jefferson's Declaration of Independence emphasizes equality of all men and their universal right to justice, liberty, self-fulfillment; July 4, Congress approves declaration, but ignores existence of slavery and unequal status of free blacks, poor white men, and women

Vocabulary

The following terms are used in Chapter 5. To understand the chapter fully, it is important that you know what each of them means.

cede to yield or formally surrender to another; to give over, as by treaty

federation a government body formed by a number of states, societies, or other units, each retaining control of its own internal affairs

boycott an organized refusal to buy or use products or to trade, for the purpose of persuading, intimidating, or coercing

chancellor of the exchequer the minister of finance in the British government, similar to the U.S. secretary of the treasury

confiscate to seize as forfeited to the public treasury; to take away property as a penalty

lobby to try to influence legislators

despotism government exercising absolute power or control; tyranny

allegiance faithfulness or loyalty to any person or thing; obligation or duty of a citizen to the government

beleaguered surrounded by an army, troubles, or other adverse conditions

requisition act of requiring or demanding; authorities taking or demanding something for military or public needs

Tories the name given during the American Revolution to Americans who remained loyal to England

vigilantes members of groups using extralegal means to control or intimidate

Identifications

After reading Chapter 5, you should be able to identify and explain the historical significance of each of the following:

King George's War

Albany Plan of Union

Seven Years' War (French and Indian War)

Neolin, Pontiac's uprising, and the Proclamation of 1763

King George III

writs of assistance and James Otis

Sugar Act and vice-admiralty courts

George Grenville

Stamp Act and Stamp Act Congress

virtual representation

Patrick Henry

Loyal Nine and Sons of Liberty

Declaratory Act

Charles Townshend and the Townshend duties (Revenue Act of 1767)

Copyright © Houghton Mifflin Company. All rights reserved.

John Wilkes

American Board of Customs Commissioners, customs racketeering

Samuel Adams

John Adams

spinning bees

Lord North

John Hancock

Crispus Attucks and the Boston Massacre

committees of correspondence

Tea Act and the Boston Tea Party

Intolerable (Coercive) Acts and Quebec Act

First Continental Congress, Suffolk Resolves, and Continental Association

minutemen, Paul Revere, and Lexington and Concord

Olive Branch Petition

Thomas Paine, *Common Sense*

Second Continental Congress and Declaration of Independence

Skill Building: Maps

On the map of eastern North America, locate each of the following and explain its importance in the imperial wars between Great Britain and France or at the beginning of the American Revolution:

Nova Scotia

Louisbourg

Ohio River and Ohio Valley

Fort Duquesne

Pittsburgh

Acadia

Quebec

Montreal

British North America under the terms of the Treaty of Paris, 1783

Fort Ticonderoga

Boston

Lexington, Massachusetts

Concord, Massachusetts

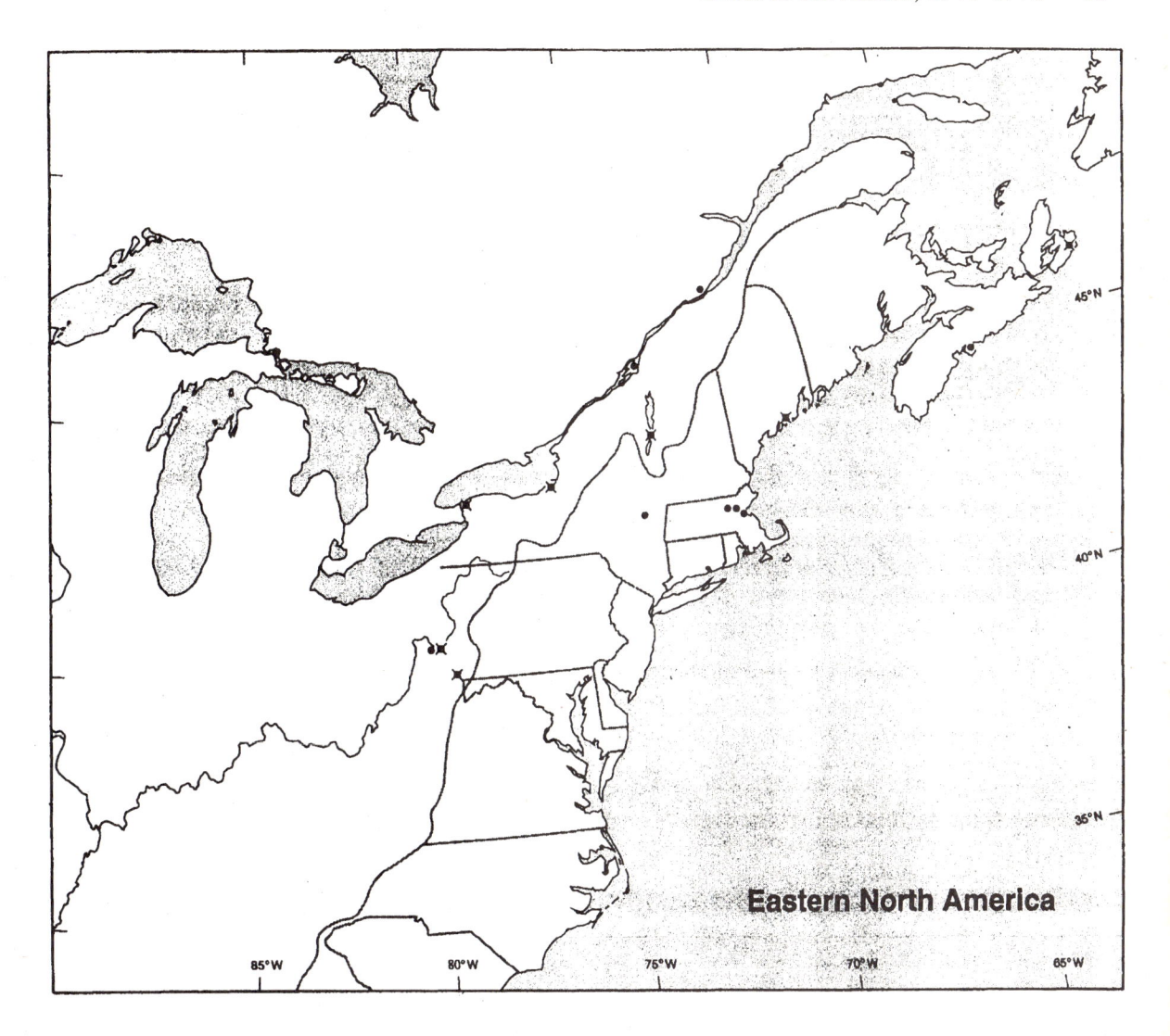

Multiple-Choice Questions

Circle the letter of the item that best completes each statement or answers the question.

1. Both the Proclamation of 1763 and the Quebec Act of 1774
   a. interfered with colonial claims to western lands.
   b. extended religious freedom to Catholics.
   c. were repealed after colonial protests.
   d. imposed new taxes on goods imported from Europe.

2. What was a chief objection that the colonists had to the British use of vice-admiralty courts?
   a. They operated without juries.
   b. They forced the accused to travel to England to stand trial.
   c. They usually imposed the death penalty for smuggling.
   d. They allowed blacks, Native Americans, and women to testify.

3. Which of the following helped convince the delegates to the Second Continental Congress that they should vote for independence?
   a. the colonists' unexpected success in clearing British troops out of New England
   b. Thomas Paine's *Common Sense*
   c. the Boston Massacre
   d. John Dickinson's *Letters from a Farmer in Pennsylvania*

4. The British claimed that Americans had virtual representation because
   a. the colonists were allowed to send delegates to the House of Commons.
   b. the colonies had their own assemblies.
   c. the members of Parliament represented all citizens of the British Empire.
   d. the colonists were represented in the Continental Congress.

5. Which of these events occurred last?
   a. the Battle of Bunker Hill
   b. the fighting at Lexington and Concord
   c. the adoption of the Declaration of Independence
   d. the Boston Massacre

6. How did the Seven Years' War differ from King William's War, Queen Anne's War, and King George's War?
   a. In the Seven Years' War, France rather than Spain was England's chief enemy.
   b. Americans participated only in the Seven Years' War.
   c. The Seven Years' War was the only one in which Native Americans sided with the French rather than the British.
   d. As a result of the Seven Years' War, France lost its empire in North America.

7. The chief reason for the repeal of the Stamp Act and the Townshend duties by Parliament was the
   a. conviction that the colonists were on the verge of revolution.
   b. pleas of Burke and Pitt to conciliate the colonists by recognizing their right to tax themselves.
   c. harmful effects of colonial boycotts and nonimportation agreements on British business.
   d. expectation that the colonial assemblies would voluntarily vote for higher taxes.

8. Americans objected to the Tea Act because
   a. it would raise the price they had to pay for tea.
   b. there was still a tax on tea, and the customs duties collected on it would be used to pay royal governors' salaries.
   c. it forced them to drink tea when they preferred coffee.
   d. it forced them to buy from the British East India Company, which sold low-quality, overpriced tea.

9. The Declaration of Independence was primarily written by
   a. John Adams.
   b. Patrick Henry.
   c. John Hancock.
   d. Thomas Jefferson.

10. John Adams did which of the following?
    a. drafted a "circular letter" to colonial legislatures condemning the Townshend duties
    b. started committees of correspondence
    c. served as the lawyer for the soldiers tried for shooting civilians in the Boston Massacre
    d. stirred up hatred of British soldiers in his *Journal of the Times*.

11. The Albany Plan of Union
    a. was vetoed by the British because it challenged royal authority.
    b. united Anglo-Americans in a loose confederation during the Seven Years' War that fell apart after the French defeat.
    c. was not implemented because of opposition by colonial legislatures, but set a precedent for future plans to unite the British mainland colonies.
    d. represented the earliest British attempt to suppress the colonial assemblies and exercise more imperial control.

12. In the Declaratory Act, Parliament stated that
    a. it had the right to legislate for the colonies in all matters, including imposing taxes.
    b. the colonists were in rebellion and therefore subject to martial law.
    c. it would repeal all of the Townshend duties except the one on tea.
    d. it would take over payment of the salaries of the royal governors and other colonial officials.

Essay Questions

1. Between 1689 and 1763, Great Britain and France and their respective allies fought four wars for supremacy in Europe and control of India and North America. Discuss the impact of those wars on America and on relations between Great Britain and its thirteen colonies.

2. In 1763 a French statesman predicted that the British would rue the day that they expelled France from North America. Did events prove the Frenchman right? How are the Seven Years' War and its outcome related to the American Revolution? Discuss.

3. One historian has written, "The British ruled the colonies for one hundred and fifty years ҏ lost them in twelve." Do you agree with this statement? Why or why not? Use as ṛ specific facts in your answer as possible.

4. Another historian claims, "A salient feature of our Revolution was that its animating, the was deeply conservative. The colonials revolted against British rule in order to keep/er as way they were, not to initiate a new era." Do you agree? Use as many facts in you possible.

5. Discuss the role of each of the following groups in the events that led to America's break with England: colonial merchants, Virginia planters, workers, sailors, artisans, and women.

Answers to Multiple-Choice Questions

1a. Yes. The Proclamation of 1763 denied colonial land claims west of the Appalachians, and the Quebec Act incorporated into the province of Quebec territories claimed by other colonies.
1b. No. The Quebec Act did that, but not the Proclamation of 1763.
1c. No. Neither law was repealed.
1d. No. Neither was a tax law.

2a. Yes. See page 86.
2b. No. Trials were held in the colonies.
2c. No. They did not.
2d. No. They did not.

3a. No. Long after the colonists drove the British out of Boston, the Continental Congress still hesitated to declare independence.
3b. Yes. See page 101.
3c. No. That happened in 1770, six years before the Declaration of Independence was adopted.
3d. No. That was a much earlier protest against taxes imposed by Parliament and in no way called for independence.

4a. No. They were not allowed to.
4b. No. The British did not recognize those assemblies as equal to Parliament.
4c. Yes. British political theory holds that members of Parliament represent the whole empire, not just the interests of the district from which they are elected.
4d. No. There was no Continental Congress at the time the British first made the argument about virtual representation, and the British regarded the Continental Congresses as illegal bodies.

5a. No. 1775
5b. No. 1775
5c. Yes. It took the delegates at the Second Continental Congress over a year after the first fighting at Lexington and Concord to decide that what they were fighting for was independence. July 4, 1776.
5d. No. 1770

6a. No. England fought France in all four wars.
6b. No. Americans participated in all four.
6c. No. In all four wars Native Americans divided, some siding with the French, some the British.
6d. Yes. The French lost all of their territory in North America to the British or the Spanish.

7a. No. The British did not believe that, and they were not yet ready for revolution.
7b. No. The advice of Pitt and Burke was generally ignored.
7c. Yes. British merchants begged Parliament to get rid of laws that were cutting their sales to the colonies by as much as 40 percent. See page 89.
7d. No. The British knew that colonial assemblies were most unlikely to do that.

No. The price of tea would actually be cheaper since the profits of the middleman would be cut out.
Yes. See pages 97–98.
No. The law did not force them to drink anything.
No. There was no complaint about the quality of the tea or the price.

9a.	No. He assisted Jefferson, but was not the main author.
9b.	No. He took no part in the writing.
9c.	No. He took no part in the writing.
9d.	Yes. See page 101.
10a.	No. That was done by his cousin, Samuel Adams.
10b.	No. See 10a.
10c.	Yes. See page 96.
10d.	No. See 10a.
11a.	No. The British were not opposed to it, and it did not challenge royal authority.
11b.	No. The plan was never put into effect.
11c.	Yes. See page 82.
11d.	No. The British were not opposed to the plan.
12a.	Yes. It was passed at the same time that Parliament repealed the Stamp Act, to make it clear to the colonists that Parliament was not giving up its claims of supremacy over all parts of the empire.
12b.	No. The colonists were not yet in rebellion.
12c.	No. The Declaratory Act was passed before the Townshend duties.
12d.	No. The British wanted to do this, but that was not what this law was about.

Copyright © Houghton Mifflin Company. All rights reserved.

CHAPTER 6
Securing Independence, Defining Nationhood, 1776–1788

Outline

I. America's First Civil War
   A. *Introduction*
      1. American Revolution is war of Americans against British
      2. American Revolution is also civil war between American Whigs (supporters of independence) and American loyalists (opponents of breaking with England)
   B. *Loyalists and Other British Sympathizers*
      1. About 20 percent of whites are loyalists (Tories)
      2. Proportion of loyalists greatest in New York and New Jersey, where leading families split between the two sides
      3. Recent British immigrants, French Canadians often loyalists
      4. 20,000 slaves escape to royal army; most Native Americans side with British
   C. *The Opposing Sides*
      1. British enter war with major advantages: outnumber Americans 11 million to 2.5 million; possess world's largest navy; have big, professional army, supplemented by Hessian mercenaries and loyalists
      2. British disadvantages: supplying troops across ocean formidable; hard to penetrate and occupy backcountry; as financial burden of war mounts, British public support for it wanes
      3. Americans mobilize manpower better than British, but one-fifth of white population is loyalist; state militias do well in guerrilla raids but wither in battle against trained British regulars
      4. Americans do not have to conquer royal army, but only hold out until British taxpayers tire of struggle
   D. *George Washington*
      1. Virginia tobacco planter, member of House of Burgesses and Continental Congress, opponent of parliamentary taxation
      2. Logical choice to command army because of his military experience in imperial wars

with France; earlier defeats teach him dangers of overconfidence and need for determination

E. *War in Earnest*
1. March 1776, British evacuate Boston, move into New York; August 1776, British badly maul Washington's army on Long Island
2. Washington retreats across New Jersey into Pennsylvania; hits back at British with sudden attacks and victories at Trenton (December 1776) and Princeton (January 1777)
3. Early 1777, British leave New Jersey; New Jersey militia harass loyalists in the state; loyalists remaining in New Jersey pledge allegiance to the Continental Congress

F. *The Turning Point*
1. October 1777, Americans foil major British offensive, attack General John Burgoyne's army near Saratoga and force its surrender
2. American victory at Saratoga convinces French that the rebels can win; February 1778, France recognizes United States; summer 1778, France goes to war with England; Spain and Holland join coalition against Great Britain
3. Coalition helps American cause by attacking British navy, forcing England to divert troops to Ireland, West Indies

G. *The Continentals Mature*
1. Fall 1777, British defeat Americans at Brandywine Creek and Germantown, Pennsylvania; British occupy Philadelphia, forcing Continental Congress to flee
2. Winter 1778, British hold Philadelphia; Washington's army freezes and drills under Friedrich von Steuben at Valley Forge, Pennsylvania
3. June 1778, British leave Philadelphia, march toward New York; Continentals catch them at Monmouth Court House, inflict heavy damage
4. British escape to New York, hold it under protection of royal navy; Washington watches from across the Hudson River

H. *Frontier Campaigns*
1. As a result of frontier victories, Americans can claim Mississippi River as their western boundary
2. 1776–1777, battles between southern whites and Cherokees; Cherokees cede lands in South Carolina, North Carolina, and Tennessee
3. George Rogers Clark's frontiersmen gain control of Ohio Valley from British and Native Americans
4. Pro-British Iroquois, under Joseph Brant, battle General John Sullivan's Continentals; Iroquois defeated near Elmira, New York; survivors flee to Canada; about one-third of Iroquois die during American Revolution

I. *Victory in the South*
1. After 1778, British focus attention on South: 1778, take Savannah, Georgia; 1780, occupy Charles Town, South Carolina
2. Lord Charles Cornwallis invades Carolina backcountry; Washington sends General

Nathaniel Greene to lead American resistance; Cornwallis leaves, heads to Virginia, establishes base at Yorktown
3. Joint French and American armies and French fleet trap Cornwallis's army at Yorktown; he surrenders October 1781
J. The Peace of Paris
1. Cornwallis's surrender forces British to negotiate peace
2. Peace talks begin in Paris, 1782; John Adams, Benjamin Franklin, John Jay represent United States
3. Terms of treaties of 1783: British recognize American independence, promise to remove all troops from U.S. territory; U.S. western boundary Mississippi River, East and West Florida go to Spain; United States promises to compensate loyalists for property losses (some states later refuse)
4. Victory costly; 5 percent of white male Americans ages sixteen to forty-five die in war

II. Revolutionary Society
A. Egalitarianism
1. War erodes class distinctions; voters will no longer elect politicians who scorn common people
2. New egalitarianism does not include propertyless white males, blacks, women, Native Americans
3. Voters feel political leaders should come from "natural aristocracy" (white men of whatever background who demonstrate virtue, accomplishments, dedication to public good)
B. A Revolution for Black Americans
1. 1776, 20 percent of U.S. population black, almost all enslaved
2. 5,000 blacks serve in Continental Army
3. Declaration of Independence's statements about equality make Whigs uneasy about slavery; by 1779 most Quakers have freed their slaves; by 1804 northern states have begun gradual emancipation
4. No southern states, where majority of blacks live, outlaw bondage; several make voluntary emancipation easier for owner; by 1790 about 5 percent of blacks in Virginia and Maryland freed
5. Most blacks remain poor laborers or tenant farmers, rely on each other for help, build independent black churches
C. White Women in the New Republic
1. Revolution brings little change in women's status; 1780s, people believe women's role is housewife and mother
2. A few women ask for equality, call for better education for females, but organized fight for women's rights does not begin until nineteenth century
D. Native Americans and the Revolution

Securing Independence, Defining Nationhood, 1776–1788 **69**

1. Newly independent nation poses threat to Native Americans' future; whites seek equal opportunity by moving west, farming on Native Americans' land
2. 1754–1783, war and uprooting reduce Native American population east of Mississippi River by almost 50 percent
3. Remaining Native Americans adopt features of white culture, participate in U.S. economy through wage labor or selling goods, but want right to practice own culture and control own communities

E. *The American Revolution and Social Change*
1. Overall distribution of wealth in nation does not change as a result of American Revolution
2. Slavery, racial injustice, subordination of women persist
3. American Revolution starts extinction of slavery in North, increases numbers and rights of free blacks, gives rise to earliest questioning of gender relations

III. Forging New Governments

A. *Tradition and Change*
1. Beliefs inherited from colonial era obstruct democratization of politics: voting and officeholding must be tied to property ownership; political parties undesirable, strife-causing factions; seats in legislatures do not need to be apportioned on basis of population
2. Revolutionary experience makes Americans wary of unchecked executive authority; they augment role of elected legislatures, frame institutions that balance interests of different classes to prevent any group from gaining absolute power

B. *From Colonies to States*
1. First state constitutions reflect conflict between democratic tendencies and conservative traditions
2. Except for Pennsylvania's, constitutions do not provide for equal-population election districts; most states reduce property qualifications for voting, but none abolish them
3. State constitutions include bills of rights, mandate frequent elections, strip governors of most powers; 1780s, many states revise constitutions to strengthen executive branch
4. Majority of states enact social reforms; for example, Virginia's Thomas Jefferson frames legislation abolishing primogeniture, entails, established church, and guaranteeing religious freedom

C. *The Articles of Confederation*
1. 1776, John Dickinson drafts Articles of Confederation; 1777, Congress sends weakened version to states for ratification; document reflects Whigs' fear of centralized power
2. Articles create unicameral Congress, one vote for each state; Congress cannot tax people, regulate interstate or foreign commerce; no executive branch; no courts
3. 1781, Articles ratified; establish a national government of very limited authority

D. Finance, Trade, and the Economy
   1. Confederation too weak to meet its greatest challenge—putting nation's finances on sound basis
   2. Robert Morris, superintendent of finance, asks for national import duty to raise money; fails to pass
   3. Congress cannot fund government or win trade concessions from Great Britain; loss of markets in British Empire causes economic depression, 1784
E. The Confederation and the West
   1. Confederate Congress passes Ordinance of 1785 and Northwest Ordinance, 1787: set successful pattern for surveying, selling, administering western lands; provide way for territories to become states; ban slavery from Northwest Territory; are Confederation's major accomplishments
   2. Congress attempts to move Native Americans farther west by negotiating treaties with their leaders; Native Americans repudiate treaties
   3. Native Americans look to British and Spanish to supply arms to resist Americans; British refuse to evacuate seven forts in Ohio Valley; Spanish supply Native Americans with arms, close port of New Orleans to western farmers
F. Shays's Rebellion
   1. 1786, Daniel Shays leads rebellion of debt-ridden Massachusetts farmers against high taxes and foreclosures
   2. Rebellion makes some Americans fear anarchy, want stronger national government to protect domestic order
   3. Urban artisans want strong government to protect them from foreign competition with high tariff; merchants want effective national government to open foreign markets for them; land speculators, westerners want powerful government to subdue Native Americans, secure western lands
   4. 1786, Annapolis convention proposes amendments to Articles of Confederation; Congress asks states to send delegates to Philadelphia meeting to amend Articles
G. The Philadelphia Convention
   1. 1787, fifty-five delegates from every state except Rhode Island assemble in Philadelphia; majority are wealthy, have legal training, share nationalist point of view
   2. James Madison's Virginia Plan proposes national government with broad powers to tax, legislate, use military force against states; specifies bicameral congress with representation in each house based on population
   3. William Patterson's New Jersey Plan calls for unicameral congress; each state has one vote regardless of population
   4. Connecticut Compromise creates bicameral legislature: equal vote for each state in Senate; proportional representation in the House
   5. Constitution finished, September 1787; vests in Congress power to levy and collect taxes, regulate interstate commerce, conduct diplomacy

Securing Independence, Defining Nationhood, 1776–1788 71

      6. Constitution balances state and federal power, interests of one social group against another, authority of one branch of national government versus another with systems of federalism, separation of powers, checks and balances
      7. Constitution recognizes and in some ways protects slavery; Constitution recognizes American people as source of political power; amendment process opens door to future democratization
      8. Philadelphia delegates arrange for ratification of Constitution by special conventions elected by people; when nine conventions have ratified, new government begins
  H. *The Struggle over Ratification*
      1. Supporters of Constitution called Federalists; those opposed, Antifederalists
      2. Antifederalists fear Constitution overcentralizes power and threatens individual liberties because bill of rights lacking
      3. Federalists: most are well-to-do; comprise most honored revolutionary leaders, such as Washington and Franklin
      4. Antifederalists: many are state and local leaders or small farmers who believe that Constitution favors urban, monied interests; include such prominent men as George Clinton, Patrick Henry, James Monroe
      5. Federalists prevail because of their vigorous leadership and promise to add bill of rights once new government starts
      6. To win support for Constitution in New York, Alexander Hamilton, James Madison, John Jay write *The Federalist Papers* (valuable commentary on Constitution by men who wrote it)

Vocabulary

The following terms are used in Chapter 6. To understand the chapter fully, it is important that you know what each of them means.

mercenaries hired soldiers serving in an army

egalitarian asserting the equality of all people

emancipation freedom from slavery

peers persons of the same civil rank or standing; equals before the law

sovereignty supreme or independent power or authority in government

republic a government in which the supreme power rests in the body of citizens entitled to vote and is exercised by representatives chosen directly or indirectly by them. Also, the head of government is nominated and/or elected rather than inheriting the position as a king

ideology the body of doctrine, myth, and symbols of a social movement, institution, social class, or large group

agrarian relating to farming, landownership, or an agricultural economy or way of life

entails legal requirements preventing an heir and all his descendants from selling or dividing an estate

Copyright © Houghton Mifflin Company. All rights reserved.

primogeniture legal requirement that, in the absence of a will, only the eldest son inherits all of a family's property

confederation a league or alliance; a body of sovereign states more or less united for common purposes

coup d'etat sudden overthrow of a government

interstate commerce business carried on in more than one state; transactions across state lines (as opposed to business done entirely within one state, or *intrastate* commerce)

anarchy a state or society without government or law; political and social disorder owing to absence of government control

ratification the act of confirming by expressing formal consent or approval

Identifications

After reading Chapter 6, you should be able to identify and explain the historical significance of each of the following:

loyalists (Tories) versus Whigs

Hessians

Marquis de Lafayette

General John Burgoyne, General Horatio Gates, and Saratoga

Friedrich von Steuben

George Rogers Clark

Joseph Brant

Yorktown

John Adams, John Jay, Benjamin Franklin, and the Peace of Paris

"natural aristocracy"

Benjamin Banneker

African Methodist Episcopal Church

Abigail Adams

"republican motherhood"

Virginia Statute for Religious Freedom, 1786

John Dickinson and the Articles of Confederation

Continentals

Ordinance of 1785 and Northwest Ordinance of 1787

Shays's Rebellion

Virginia Plan, New Jersey Plan, and Connecticut Compromise

checks and balances, separation of powers, federalism

Federalists versus Antifederalists

John Jay, Alexander Hamilton, James Madison, and *The Federalist Papers*

Skill Building: Maps

1. On the map of eastern North America, locate each of the following and explain its importance in the American Revolution.

Boston

New York City

Long Island

Trenton, New Jersey

Princeton, New Jersey

Albany, New York

Philadelphia, Pennsylvania

Saratoga, New York

Brandywine Creek and Germantown, Pennsylvania

Valley Forge, Pennsylvania

Monmouth, New Jersey

Tennessee

Kentucky

Ohio River

Elmira, New York

Savannah, Georgia

Charles Town, South Carolina

Yorktown, Virginia

2. Draw in the boundaries of the United States as set by the Peace of Paris in 1783. Add the boundaries of the Northwest Territory created by the Ordinance of 1785 and the Northwest Ordinance of 1787.

Eastern North America

Multiple-Choice Questions

Circle the letter of the item that best completes each statement or answers the question.

1. Which of the following was *least* likely to be a loyalist during the American Revolution?
   a. a Boston merchant
   b. a recent immigrant to the colonies from Great Britain
   c. a Virginia slave
   d. a Catholic French-Canadian

Securing Independence, Defining Nationhood, 1776–1788

2. Which statement about the men who wrote the U.S. Constitution is correct?
   a. Most were wealthy men who were convinced that unless the national government was strengthened, the country would fall victim to foreign aggression.
   b. Most doubted that a republic could effectively govern a nation as large as the United States.
   c. Most were men in their fifties and sixties who distrusted the younger revolutionaries.
   d. They wanted to get on with creating a democratic government that would enforce their belief that all men are created equal.

3. The Northwest Ordinance
   a. left the decision of whether to permit slavery in the territory to those who settled there.
   b. was the first law passed by Congress after the new federal government created by the Constitution started.
   c. removed Native Americans and guaranteed white settlers the right to buy land in the territory.
   d. forbade slavery in the Northwest Territory and set the pattern by which a territory could become a state.

4. The British justified their refusal to evacuate their military forts in the Ohio Valley after the American Revolution by pointing to America's failure to
   a. stop Native American attacks against Canada.
   b. pay for wartime damage to British shipping.
   c. return or pay for loyalists' property.
   d. allow British goods to enter the United States duty-free.

5. Which of the following represented the most serious difficulty facing American commercial interests at the end of the American Revolution?
   a. loss of the protection of the British Navy
   b. British restrictions on trade with the West Indies
   c. decreased demand for American goods in Europe
   d. France's refusal to sign a commercial treaty

6. Shays's Rebellion was provoked by
   a. retention of the Northwest posts by Great Britain.
   b. the failure of the government to protect frontier settlements from attacks by Native Americans.
   c. an excise tax imposed by Congress on whiskey.
   d. the heavy burden of taxes on the farmers of western Massachusetts.

7. The Battle of Saratoga is significant because it
   a. showed the lack of discipline in the Continental Army.
   b. ended the fighting in the North.
   c. brought French diplomatic recognition and a military alliance.
   d. broke the British will to continue to fight.

8. The Antifederalists' greatest achievement was to
   a. force the Federalists to agree to add a bill of rights to the Constitution.
   b. convince New York and Virginia to turn over their western lands to the new national government.
   c. delay ratification of the Constitution until a section guaranteeing all white men the right to vote and hold office was added.
   d. force the Federalists to bestow citizenship under the new government to free blacks.

9. Who was the author of Virginia's Statute for Religious Freedom and bills abolishing entails and primogeniture?
   a. George Washington
   b. Richard Henry Lee
   c. Thomas Jefferson
   d. Patrick Henry

10. Which of the following is true of the state constitutions adopted during the American Revolution?
    a. They abolished property and taxpaying qualifications for voting.
    b. They provided for election districts with equal population.
    c. They lacked bills of rights.
    d. They provided for weak executives and frequent elections.

11. Which of the following statements about the social changes produced by the American Revolution is correct?
    a. It brought about a considerable redistribution of wealth and property within the thirteen states.
    b. It set in motion the gradual ending of slavery everywhere in the North.
    c. It enhanced the political rights of women, including allowing those with independent wealth to vote.
    d. It convinced the authors of state constitutions to remove all property requirements for white male voters.

12. Which of the following men was both an author of the U.S. Constitution and an outspoken supporter of its ratification?
    a. Thomas Jefferson
    b. Patrick Henry
    c. James Madison
    d. George Clinton

Essay Questions

1. Besides being a war for independence from Great Britain, the American Revolution was also a civil war of American against American and a war of Native Americans to defend their homelands. Discuss and illustrate this statement with as many facts as possible.

2. Discuss the advantages and disadvantages the British and the Americans each had in fighting the American Revolution. What do you think accounts for the Americans' ultimate victory?

3. Discuss the social, economic, and political changes within the thirteen states produced by the American Revolution. Be sure to consider slavery, status of women, property distribution, voting rights, and religion in your answer.

4. Discuss the United States' domestic and foreign difficulties under the Articles of Confederation. What did the government accomplish under the Articles?

5. Discuss the backgrounds and political beliefs of the men who wrote the U.S. Constitution. What did they hope to accomplish by establishing this Constitution?

Answers to Multiple-Choice Questions

1a. Yes. See page 105.
1b. No. Recent British immigrants tended to identify with their former homeland.
1c. No. Many Virginia slaves tried to escape and aid the British after the royal governor, Lord Dunmore, promised them freedom if they helped the crown.
1d. No. In the Quebec Act (1774), the British guaranteed French Catholics religious freedom, a right they feared the mostly Protestant American revolutionaries would not respect.

2a. Yes. See pages 124-125.
2b. No. They believed in a republic.
2c. No. They were relatively young and had been leaders of the Revolution.
2d. No. Many believed the country was suffering from excess democracy or mob rule.

3a. No. It banned slavery from the territory.
3b. No. It was passed by Congress under the Articles of Confederation, before the Constitution was drafted and ratified.
3c. No. Not a part of the Ordinance.
3d. Yes. See page 122.

4a. No. That was not a problem.
4b. No. Not an issue between the United States and Britain.
4c. Yes. Americans had promised in the treaty ending the Revolution to make such payments, but many of the states refused to enforce this provision. See page 123.
4d. No. British goods were often entering duty-free.

5a. No. Not a threat to commerce.
5b. Yes. The West Indies had been one of the best customers for colonial produce, and now the British kept out most American exports. See page 122.
5c. No. The demand was the same.
5d. No. France was not discriminating against American trade.

6a. No. Had nothing to do with that.
6b. No. Not a dispute about Indians.
6c. No. That would cause a later protest in Western Pennsylvania during President Washington's administration.
6d. Yes. See page 124.

Copyright © Houghton Mifflin Company. All rights reserved.

7a. No. It was a major victory for the Americans.
7b. No. There were subsequent battles.
7c. Yes. The victory convinced the French that the colonists had a chance to beat the British, and so were worth helping. See page 111.
7d. No. The British continued fighting for several more years.

8a. Yes. See page 129.
8b. No. The dispute between Federalists and Antifederalists was not about western lands.
8c. No. No such guarantee went into the Constitution.
8d. No. The Constitution did not define citizenship. That was first done in the 14th Amendment.

9a. No. He was not.
9b. No. See 9a.
9c. Yes. See page 120.
9d. No. See 9a.

10a. No. None of them went that far, though several reduced the amount of property and/or taxes required.
10b. No. Most of them did not try to equalize population in election districts.
10c. No. All of them had bills of rights.
10d. Yes. This reflected the American fear of executive power because of their past experiences with royal governors. See page 119.

11a. No. Property confiscated from wealthy loyalists ended up in the hands of equally wealthy Whigs.
11b. Yes. See page 115.
11c. No. Women gained almost no new political rights.
11d. No. That did not happen.
12a. No. Jefferson did not attend the Constitutional Convention, had no hand in writing the Constitution, and was worried that it might create too strong a central government.
12b. No. Henry was an outspoken Antifederalist.
12c. Yes. Madison was one of the main framers of the Constitution and one of the authors of *The Federalist Papers*, written in support of ratification. See pages 125 and 129.
12d. No. Clinton was a leading New York Antifederalist.

CHAPTER 7
Launching the New Republic, 1789–1800

Outline

I. **Constitutional Government Takes Shape**
   A. *Introduction*
      1. March 1789, men elected to Congress under the Constitution gather in new national capital, New York
      2. Lawmakers must fill in details in areas left vague in Constitution: president's cabinet, national courts, rights of individual
   B. *Defining the Presidency*
      1. Constitution mentions executive departments only in passing; through legislation Congress establishes first cabinet
      2. Cabinet consists of four departments headed by secretaries of state, treasury, and war, and attorney general; Washington balances appointments between southerners and northerners
      3. Washington reluctantly accepts reelection to presidency in 1792
   C. *National Justice and the Bill of Rights*
      1. Constitution authorizes Congress to provide for federal courts below Supreme Court; Congress creates federal court system with Judiciary Act of 1789
      2. James Madison drafts and Congress passes first ten amendments that become the Bill of Rights; ratified December 1791
      3. First eight amendments protect individual rights: freedom of speech, press, assembly, and religion, and procedures for fair trial and punishment; Ninth and Tenth Amendments reserve to people and states powers not specifically granted to federal government by Constitution

II. **National Economic Policy and Its Consequences**
   A. *Alexander Hamilton and His Objectives*
      1. Secretary of the Treasury Alexander Hamilton has great influence over President Washington
      2. Hamilton's goals: to strengthen United States against foreign enemies, prevent disunion; to achieve goals, he wants to establish the nation's credit, promote

economic self-sufficiency through industrialization and strong merchant marine
3. Hamilton believes federal government's survival depends on gaining support of politically influential citizens by benefiting them economically

B. *Report on the Public Credit*
1. January 1790, Hamilton sends his Report on Public Credit to Congress; proposes that federal government quickly pay off foreign debt; domestic holders of American Revolution war bonds issued by Continental Congress and states can exchange them at full value for new U.S. government bonds carrying 4 percent interest
2. Hamilton urges Congress to maintain perpetual debt, issue new interest-bearing bonds as old ones paid out
3. Hamilton foresees that permanent debt and assumption of state debt will tie creditor classes to federal government, giving them stake in its survival and economic health
4. James Madison and others in Congress oppose Hamilton's plan because most of American Revolution war bond holders are rich speculators who have bought bonds for a fraction of their value from original owners
5. Hamilton convinces Congress to enact his policies; trades Virginia votes for assumption of state debt for northern votes to locate permanent U.S. capital on Potomac
6. Adoption of these measures improves U.S. credit rating

C. *Reports on the Bank and Manufactures*
1. December 1790, Hamilton asks Congress to charter national bank, with government owning one-fifth of its stock, and private individuals, four-fifths
2. Bank's purposes: make profit for private shareholders, serve as depository for federal tax receipts, make low-interest loans to government, issue notes to circulate as national currency, regulate practices of state banks, provide credit to expand U.S. economy
3. Report also proposes encouraging manufacturing and other industries by enactment of protective tariffs and subsidies
4. Thomas Jefferson and Madison oppose Hamilton's permanent government debt, national bank, and protective tariffs
5. Jefferson, Madison, and others argue Hamilton's proposals favor a rich, creditor elite at expense of rest of people
6. Congress passes bank charter bill; Washington worries about its constitutionality, asks Hamilton and Jefferson to write opinions
7. Hamilton: bank charter constitutional under "necessary and proper" clause and "loose interpretation"; Jefferson: charter unconstitutional under "strict interpretation," Congress may not do anything not specified in Constitution
8. February 1791, Washington signs bank charter bill
9. Congress rejects high protective tariff; aids U.S. shipping by imposing lower import duty on goods carried on U.S.-owned vessels

D. *Hamilton's Legacy*
1. Beneficiaries of Hamilton's policies (speculators, merchants, urban entrepreneurs)

Launching the New Republic, 1789–1800 81

        rally behind Washington administration, call themselves Federalists
- 2. Federalists strongest in New England, New Jersey, South Carolina; many adherents in Pennsylvania and New York
- 3. Agricultural interests of South, West, Middle Atlantic states see no gains for themselves in Hamilton's program; call for return to true republicanism

E. *The Whiskey Rebellion*
- 1. March 1791, Congress imposes excise tax on domestically produced whiskey to pay for Hamilton's program
- 2. Western Pennsylvania farmers oppose tax because it eliminates their income from selling corn liquor; July 1794, they attack U.S. marshal serving summonses on delinquent taxpayers
- 3. Washington and Hamilton decide to crush Whiskey Rebellion forcefully to demonstrate that citizens must obey federal law, can resist only by constitutional means

III. The United States on the World Stage

A. *Spanish Power in the Far West*
- 1. Late eighteenth century, Spanish ambitions in western North America revive
- 2. Spain strengthens its hold on New Mexico and Texas by improving relations and trade with Native Americans
- 3. Spain spreads settlements and missions up the coast of California
- 4. Spain hopes to counter growing presence of Russia, Britain, and United States in Pacific Northwest and fur trade with China

B. *The Trans-Appalachian Frontier*
- 1. Greatest danger to nation comes from Native Americans resisting westward movement and from British and Spanish helping Native Americans and attempting to detach West from United States
- 2. 1791–1796, Vermont, Kentucky, Tennessee become states
- 3. Washington's attempts to pacify and integrate eastern tribes fail; United States continues to pressure Native Americans to cede their lands and move west

C. *France and Factional Politics*
- 1. 1789, French Revolution begins; 1793, France goes to war against Great Britain and Spain
- 2. Americans divided on foreign policy: South and West pro-French, hope war will weaken Great Britain and Spain and stop their troublemaking in West; northern merchants pro-British, dependent on good relations with England to carry on shipping and trade
- 3. 1793, French ambassador Edmond Genet tries to get United States to help France; recruits U.S. volunteers to seize New Orleans, St. Augustine, and British ships at sea
- 4. April 1793, Washington declares U.S. neutrality

D. *The British Crisis*

1. British retaliate against U.S. privateers by seizing U.S. merchant ships, impressing seamen, inciting Native Americans in Ohio Valley, building Fort Miami (near Toledo, Ohio); Spanish erect Fort San Fernando in Tennessee
2. 1794, Anthony Wayne defeats Native Americans at Battle of Fallen Timbers (near Fort Miami); 1795, tribes sign Treaty of Greenville, opening Ohio to white settlement
3. Great Britain and United States sign Jay's Treaty: war averted, and British promise to evacuate forts in Ohio Valley but make no concessions on impressment or on interference with U.S. ships; 1795, Senate ratifies treaty by one vote
4. 1796, Treaty of San Lorenzo (Pinckney's Treaty): Spain gives U.S. citizens unrestricted use of Mississippi River, withdraws forts from U.S. soil, agrees to thirty-first parallel as southern boundary
5. Despite Washington's foreign-policy accomplishments, by 1796 Americans divided on policies toward Great Britain, France, Spain

IV. Battling for the Nation's Soul

A. *Ideological Confrontation*
1. Federalists horrified at radicalism of French Revolution, suspicious of common people and direct democracy; believe government must be allied with upper class
2. Jefferson, Madison, many white southerners retain sympathy for revolutionary France, do not fear popular participation in politics, rouse ordinary citizens against Federalists through newspapers
3. 1793–1794, popular discontent with Federalists leads to organization of Democratic (Republican) societies

B. *The Republican Party*
1. By 1793 Washington is identified with Federalists; Jefferson resigns from cabinet to lead opposition party
2. Federalist and Republican newspapers trade charges, stimulate popular interest in politics
3. 1796, Washington decides to retire; farewell address warns against political parties and entangling alliances with European countries

C. *The Election of 1796*
1. Republicans win support of Democratic societies, workingmen's clubs, French and Irish immigrants
2. Federalist presidential candidate, John Adams; Republican, Jefferson
3. Federalists win big in New England; Republicans in South; swing states: New York goes Federalist, Pennsylvania, Republican; Federalists narrowly gain presidency and control of Congress
4. Jefferson, runner-up, becomes vice president under provision of original Constitution, later changed by Twelfth Amendment

D. *The French Crisis*

1. France seizes U.S. ships; hoping to avoid war, President Adams sends peace commission to Paris
2. XYZ Affair: French government agents demand bribe as price for negotiations; U.S. outraged, anti-French, anti-Republican backlash in U.S. public opinion
3. 1798, Federalists gain seats in Congress; fight undeclared naval war with France; size of U.S. army triples

E. The Alien and Sedition Act
1. 1798, Federalist Congress passes Alien and Sedition Acts to silence and weaken Republican opponents: impose fourteen-year waiting period for naturalization so Irish immigrants cannot vote for Republicans; make it crime to speak, write, print unfavorable comments about president and party in power
2. Federalists prosecute and jail Republican journalists and politicians; 1798–1799, Madison and Jefferson fight back with states' rights Virginia and Kentucky resolutions
3. Resolutions claim state governments can interpose themselves between their residents and enforcement of unconstitutional federal laws; states can nullify unconstitutional acts of federal government

F. The Election of 1800
1. Republicans nominate Jefferson for president, Aaron Burr, vice president
2. Federalists split between "High Federalist" followers of Hamilton and backers of President Adams; High Federalists angry with Adams for reopening talks with France and removing threat of war
3. Adams loses; Jefferson and Burr tie; election thrown into House of Representatives, which chooses Jefferson

V. Economic and Social Change

A. The Household Economy
1. In New England, economy after the Revolution begins shift from household family self-sufficiency to early stages of home manufacturing
2. Merchants traveling into countryside supply farm families with raw materials which they turn into cloth, shoes, nails and other manufactured products; merchants collect output from farm families and pay them cash
3. Merchants behind these new ventures in the 1780s and 1790s also opening the first banks and stock exchanges, preaching need for United States to industrialize, and supporting Hamilton's economic policies

B. Indians in the New Republic
1. By 1795 eastern tribes much reduced in population and territory by battle, famine, disease
2. Many Native Americans sink into alcoholism and despair; 1799, Seneca prophet Handsome Lake tries to combat liquor and encourages Iroquois to farm; such cultural changes resisted, come slowly

84 Chapter 7

  C. *Redefining the Color Line*
  1. Improving status of U.S. blacks and growing antislavery sentiment stimulated by American Revolution regress in 1790s
  2. States strip free blacks of right to vote; Congress limits naturalization to white immigrants; 1793, passes Fugitive Slave Law
  3. Reasons for revival of racism and slavery: white fears generated by Saint Domingue (Haiti) and Gabriel slave revolts; British textile industry's demand for cotton; Eli Whitney's invention of cotton gin

Vocabulary

The following terms are used in Chapter 7. To understand the chapter fully, it is important that you know what each of them means.

speculator a person trading in land, commodities, or stocks and bonds in the hope of profiting from changes in the market price; one who engages in business transactions involving considerable risk but offering large gains

secession formal withdrawal from an association, as in the case of states withdrawing from the union

entrepreneurs persons who develop and carry out new economic enterprises

tariff a tax imposed on imported products

excise tax a tax levied on goods and services manufactured, sold, or offered within the country

privateer a privately owned and manned armed vessel commissioned by a government in time of war to fight the enemy, especially its commercial shipping

impress to force into service, as with a seaman; to seize or take for public use or service

constituents the voters and residents of a district, state, or country who an elected official represents

abomination an object greatly disliked or hated; a horror

anomaly something abnormal or unusual

demagoguery the methods or practices of a demagogue—that is, a leader who uses popular passions or prejudices for his or her own interests; the methods or practices of an unprincipled popular orator or agitator

partisan a supporter of a political party or cause; actions motivated by support of a political party or cause

electorate the body of persons entitled to vote in an election

sedition incitement of discontent or rebellion against the government; action or language promoting such discontent or rebellion

Identifications

After reading Chapter 7, you should be able to identify and explain the historical significance of each of the following:

Judiciary Act of 1789

Bill of Rights

Hamilton's Report on the Public Credit, 1790

James Madison

Hamilton's Report on a National Bank

Hamilton's Report on Manufactures

strict versus loose interpretation, and the "necessary and proper" clause of the Constitution

Federalists versus Republicans

Whiskey Rebellion

citizen Edmond Genet

Anthony Wayne, Battle of Fallen Timbers, and Treaty of Greenville

Jay's Treaty

Treaty of San Lorenzo (Pinckney's Treaty)

Washington's farewell address

XYZ Affair

Quasi-War with France

Alien and Sedition Acts, 1798

Virginia and Kentucky resolutions, 1798

interposition and nullification

"High Federalists"

election of 1800

Handsome Lake

Fugitive Slave Law, 1793

Saint Domingue (Haiti) slave uprising

Gabriel Prosser and Gabriel's Rebellion, 1800

Eli Whitney and the cotton gin

Skill Building: Maps

On the map of the eastern half of the United States, locate and explain the historical importance of each place in the period 1789–1800.

Fort Miami (Toledo, Ohio)

Fort San Fernando (Memphis, Tennessee)

Ohio River

Northwest Territory

Appalachian Mountains

Chapter 7

New Orleans
Mississippi River
Vermont
Kentucky
Tennessee
thirty-first parallel

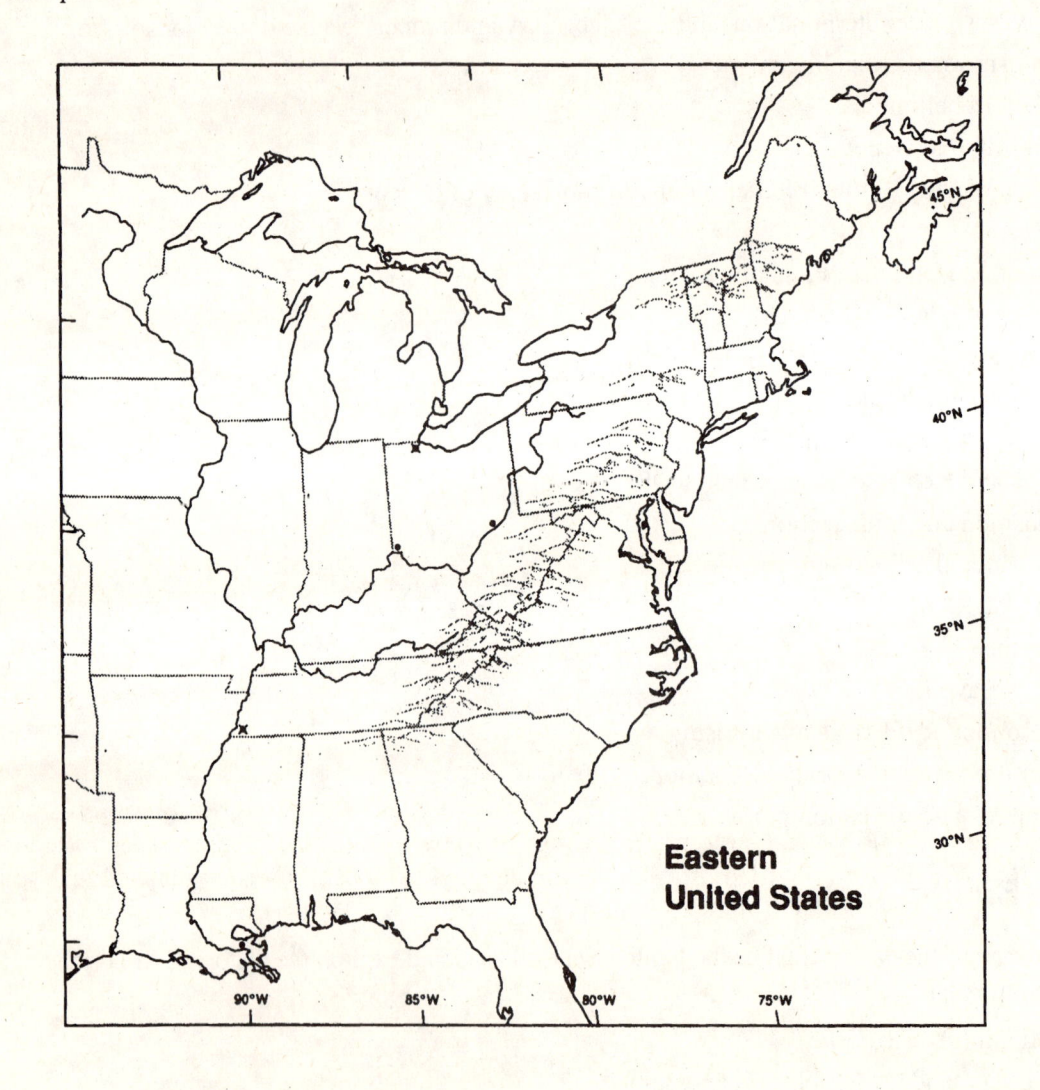

Eastern United States

Multiple-Choice Questions

Circle the letter of the item that best completes each statement or answers the question.

1. The main purpose of the Alien and Sedition Acts was to
   a. publicize the activities of French revolutionaries in the United States.
   b. strengthen the policy of neutrality.
   c. strengthen the Republican party.
   d. silence and suppress the Republican opposition.

2. Hamilton wanted the federal government to take over in full the American Revolution war debt of the Continental Congress and the states because he believed that
   a. doing so would cause a heavy loss to speculators in certificates.
   b. the payment of all such obligations was guaranteed in the Constitution.
   c. doing so would cause well-to-do creditors to favor the new federal government and the extension of its powers.
   d. the states unanimously favored such a policy.

3. Hamilton's financial program was designed to do which of the following?
   a. gain the support of the commercial upper class for the new national government
   b. establish the credit of the United States at home and abroad
   c. encourage industrialization in the United States
   d. all of the above

4. Hamilton's national bank
   a. provoked the first clear-cut argument over the strict versus loose interpretation of the Constitution.
   b. was a fully government-owned and -operated institution.
   c. helped the United States retire its old revolutionary debt as quickly as possible.
   d. all of the above

5. The XYZ Affair
   a. arose out of the French government's demand for a bribe as the price for negotiations.
   b. increased the popularity of the Republican party and hurt the fortunes of the Federalists.
   c. was provoked by Hamilton to increase the popularity of the Washington administration.
   d. arose out of the Whiskey Rebellion.

6. The Virginia and Kentucky resolutions
   a. attacked the Alien and Sedition Acts.
   b. were written by James Madison and Thomas Jefferson.
   c. claimed the right of a state to protect its people from unconstitutional federal laws.
   d. all of the above

7. Speculators took advantage of which of these Federalist measures?
   a. the excise tax
   b. the refunding of the national debt by paying full face value of American Revolution war bonds
   c. the tariff
   d. placing the federal capital on land donated by Virginia and Maryland

8. Which action of President John Adams angered the "High Federalists"?
   a. his handling of the XYZ Affair
   b. his signing of the Alien and Sedition Acts
   c. his decision to improve relations with France between 1799 and 1800
   d. his request for a larger army

9. Which of these people would probably *not* support Thomas Jefferson's Republican party?
   a. a Virginia planter
   b. a Boston merchant
   c. a western Pennsylvania farmer
   d. a recent Irish immigrant

10. Which of the following people scored a victory over the Native Americans that opened Ohio to white settlement and won a promise by the British to evacuate forts in the Northwest Territory?
    a. Gabriel Prosser
    b. Anthony Wayne
    c. Handsome Lake
    d. Samuel Slater

11. Which of the following men drafted the first ten amendments to the Constitution that became the Bill of Rights?
    a. Thomas Jefferson
    b. Alexander Hamilton
    c. James Madison
    d. John Adams

12. Why did farmers in western Pennsylvania object to the excise tax on whiskey?
    a. It was imposed by the British Parliament, in which they had no representation.
    b. They turned their bulky grain into whiskey to make it easier to ship to market, and the tax wiped out the little profit they made.
    c. They feared that the proceeds would be used to pay higher salaries to corrupt government officials.
    d. Whiskey was their favorite drink, and the tax made it too expensive for them to afford.

Essay Questions

1. Discuss the rise of political parties in the United States. Did the Constitution provide for political parties? If not, when and why did the first two parties develop? Who led and supported each party?

2. Discuss the economic and financial programs of Secretary of the Treasury Alexander Hamilton. What did they include? What was Hamilton trying to accomplish? How and why did his programs politically divide Americans?

3. Discuss the deteriorating positions of African-Americans and Native Americans after the American Revolution. How do you account for the deterioration? What major changes or events marked the declining status of each group?

4. Explain how differences over foreign policy in the period 1789–1800 encouraged the development of political parties and partisanship.

5. Discuss the dangers faced by the nation during the Federalist era (1789–1800) and the ways it overcame or survived them. In your answer, be sure to include conflict among social, economic, and sectional interest groups; challenges from foreign nations; and threats to individual liberties and the Bill of Rights.

Answers to Multiple-Choice Questions

1a. No. Not what these laws aimed at.
1b. No. They were passed by a Federalist-dominated Congress out to weaken the opposition party, not keep the United States neutral toward France and Britain.
1c. No. Just the opposite. Federalists wanted to weaken the Republicans.
1d. Yes. See page 145.

2a. No. It would, in fact, be very favorable to speculators.
2b. No. The Constitution said nothing about this.
2c. Yes. See page 135.
2d. No. States that had already paid off much of their debt opposed federal assumption.

3a. No. That was one objective, but there were others.
3b. No. See 3a.
3c. No. See 3a.
3d. Yes. Hamilton wished to accomplish all of these objectives. See pages 135-136.

4a. Yes. When Washington asked his cabinet members, Secretary of State Jefferson and Secretary of Treasury Hamilton, to write him opinions on the constitutionality of the bank charter bill, they produced the first clear-cut arguments for strict v. loose interpretation. See page 136.
4b. No. Four-fifths of the stock would be owned by private investors.
4c. No. Hamilton believed it was a good thing for the U.S. Government to keep in permanent debt to its wealthier citizens.
4d. No. Since 4b and 4c are false.

5a. Yes. See page 144.
5b. No. Just the opposite; the Republicans became unpopular for being the party too soft on the offending French.

Copyright © Houghton Mifflin Company. All rights reserved.

5c. No. Hamilton was not involved in the incident.
5d. No. A separate issue.

6a. No. Because while this is true, so are 6b and 6c. Therefore, the answer has to be 6d, "all of the above."
6b. No. See 6a.
6c. No. See 6a.
6d. Yes. See pages 145-146.

7a. No. That didn't affect them one way or the other.
7b. Yes. Speculators had bought up old revolutionary war bonds for as little as ten to fifteen cents on the dollar and would now get the full face value of the bond.
7c. No. That was meant to help domestic manufacturers.
7d. No. That was agreed to in order to get southern votes for federal assumption of state debts.

8a. No. They were glad he exploited it to make the Republicans look bad.
8b. No. The "High Federalists" were the ones who pushed those laws through Congress.
8c. Yes. Since this weakened the position of the Federalists and improved the standing of the Republicans in the election of 1800. See page 146.
8d. No. The Federalists liked that and thought they might use that army to suppress Republican supporters at home.

9a. No. Most Virginia planters supported the Jeffersonian Republicans.
9b. Yes. Northern businessmen saw Federalist (Hamiltonian) economic policies as favorable to their interests, and disliked Jefferson's pro-agriculture, anti-commerce and manufacturing, and pro-French Revolution attitudes.
9c. No. Western and southern farmers and planters were among Jefferson's main supporters.
9d. No. Most of the recent Irish and French immigrants voted for the Republicans.

10a. No. Prosser led a slave rebellion.
10b. Yes. See page 141.
10c. No. He was a Seneca Indian who tried to get his people to renounce drinking and adopt an agricultural way of life.
10d. No. He was important in furthering the industrialization of the United States.

11a. No. He was not elected to Congress.
11b. No. He did not serve in Congress.
11c. Yes. As a member of the House of Representatives, he drafted and introduced the amendments which were passed by Congress and then sent to the states for ratification. See page 133.
11d. No. See 11a and 11b.

12a. No. It was imposed by the Congress of the United States.
12b. Yes. See page 137.
12c. No. Not what the proceeds were earmarked for.
12d. No. The farmers were making the whiskey.

CHAPTER 8
Jeffersonianism and the Era of Good Feelings

Outline

I. **The Age of Jefferson**
   A. *Introduction*
      1. Thomas Jefferson's background: slaveowner, aristocrat, champion of rights of common man, lawyer, governor of Virginia, secretary of state, vice president
      2. Jefferson's beliefs: liberty; republics; frugal federal government with limited power; more power in state governments that are closer to the people; best citizens of a republic are educated small farmers; cities and their landless urban masses are dangerous to liberty; be practical rather than holding fast to abstract principles
   B. *Jefferson's "Revolution"*
      1. Jefferson sees his election as a revolution to restore liberty, stop drift to despotism
      2. Jefferson and Congress repeal internal taxes, cut federal expenditures
      3. Jefferson sends U.S. naval expeditions against Barbary pirates rather than pay tribute
      4. Jefferson and Congress reduce U.S. army
   C. *Jefferson and the Judiciary*
      1. Judiciary Act of 1801 creates sixteen new federal judgeships; Adams, before leaving presidency, fills all with Federalists ("midnight appointments")
      2. Republican Congress repeals Judiciary Act of 1801
      3. Chief Justice John Marshall, in *Marbury* v. *Madison,* for first time declares act of Congress unconstitutional, establishing right of judicial review
      4. Jefferson does not oppose judicial review but objects to Federalist use of the courts to benefit their party
      5. Jefferson and Republicans attempt to remove two Federalist judges by impeachment; obtain conviction of only one
   D. *The Louisiana Purchase*
      1. Napoleon acquires Louisiana Territory; dreams of French empire in Americas; changes plans when French cannot reconquer Haiti
      2. Despite qualms about constitutionality, Jefferson buys Louisiana Territory from France for $15,000,000

3. Importance of the Louisiana Purchase: removes a major European power from U.S. western border; gives the United States control of New Orleans and the mouth of the Mississippi; doubles the nation's size; provides good land for U.S. farmers for generations

E. *The Lewis and Clark Expedition*
1. Jefferson asks Congress to appropriate money for expedition across North American continent to explore the Louisiana Purchase, map the region, and bring back scientific and other useful information
2. Expedition, led by Meriwether Lewis and William Clark, leaves St. Louis in 1804; goes all the way to the Pacific coast before returning
3. Expedition returns with wealth of scientific information and stimulates interest in the West

F. *The Election of 1804*
1. Republicans renominate Jefferson; replace Aaron Burr with George Clinton for vice president
2. Jefferson wins by big majority over Federalist Charles C. Pinckney
3. Accomplishments of Jefferson's first term: acquiring the vast Louisiana Territory, paying off much of the public debt, keeping the country at peace

II. **The Gathering Storm**

A. *Introduction*
1. Renewed war in Europe
2. Problems of Jefferson's second term: breakdown of Republican party unity; British and French interference with U.S. neutral rights to freedom of seas and trade with all nations

B. *Jefferson's Coalition Fragments*
1. Factionalism in the Republican party: Burr schemes to detach southwestern states from the country
2. Jefferson orders Burr's arrest, trial for treason; with help from Chief Justice John Marshall, Burr acquitted

C. *Jefferson and the Quids*
1. John Randolph and the Quids denounce Jefferson for compromising republican virtue
2. Criticize Jefferson's handling of the Yazoo land claims

D. *The Suppression of U.S. Trade*
1. War resumes between Great Britain and France
2. British Orders in Council and French counter orders interference with U.S. trade
3. Britain and France seize U.S. ships; British often do this right off U.S. coast

E. *Impressment*
1. British impress sailors from U.S. merchant ships

Jeffersonianism and the Era of Good Feelings

   2. In *Chesapeake-Leopard* Affair (1807), British attack U.S. naval frigate, impress four sailors; public opinion indignant
 F. *The Embargo Act*
   1. Jefferson attempts to make Great Britain and France respect America's neutral rights by prohibiting American ships from carrying exports abroad
   2. Embargo Act fails and has adverse effects on the United States
   3. Embargo stimulates U.S. manufacturing
 G. *The Election of 1808*
   1. Republican James Madison beats Federalist Charles C. Pinckney
   2. Federalists revive owing to unpopularity of the embargo and active campaigning of younger Federalists
 H. *The Failure of Peaceable Coercion*
   1. Madison, like Jefferson, believes in primacy of agriculture
   2. Madison attempts to make Great Britain respect U.S. neutrality by denying U.S. produce to British West Indies; policy fails, West Indies get food from Canada
   3. Madison and Congress try further economic coercion on Great Britain and France with Non-Intercourse Act (1809) and Macon's Bill No. 2 (1810); U.S. trade not important enough to Great Britain or France to change their policies
   4. Pressure put on Madison by militant Republicans who want more aggressive policy toward Britain and France
   5. Election of 1810: many "war hawks" from South and West, led by Henry Clay, win seats in Congress
 I. *Tecumseh and the Prophet*
   1. War hawks want to force Great Britain out of Canada and Spain out of Florida
   2. War hawks and westerners believe British are arming and inciting Native Americans on the frontier
   3. Shawnee chief Tecumseh and his half-brother, the Prophet, attempt to unite the tribes of Ohio and Indiana against white settlers
   4. Initially, they have no connection with British, but after William Henry Harrison attacks the Prophet's town and wins the Battle of Tippecanoe, Tecumseh joins forces with Great Britain
 J. *Congress Votes for War*
   1. June 1, 1812, Madison sends war message to Congress
   2. Republicans vote for war; Federalists from New England and New York against
   3. Madison leads the country into war because he believes impressment and British ships hovering off U.S. coast violate our neutral rights; continuing British restriction on U.S. shipping causing recession in South and West; British intend to ruin United States as commercial rival

III. The War of 1812
 A. *On to Canada*

94   Chapter 8

   1. U.S. attempts to conquer Canada fail
   2. British take Detroit; Oliver H. Perry scores victory on Lake Erie
   3. United States retakes Detroit; William Henry Harrison wins in 1813 at Battle of the Thames, Tecumseh killed
  B. *The British Offensive*
   1. British fail to cut off New England from the rest of the states
   2. British capture Washington, D.C. and burn it
   3. After British fail to take Baltimore, they end campaign
  C. *The Treaty of Ghent*
   1. December 1814, treaty signed in Ghent, Belgium, restores the prewar status quo
   2. 1815, Andrew Jackson wins postwar U.S. victory at Battle of New Orleans
  D. *The Hartford Convention*
   1. Unpopularity of the war in the Northeast contributes to the Federalist revival in the election of 1812; antiwar Republicans and Federalists run DeWitt Clinton for president against Madison; Madison wins election but loses most of New England, New York, New Jersey
   2. In protest against the war, Federalists convene Hartford Convention in fall 1814; pass resolutions aimed at strengthening New England's power within Union
   3. Return of peace and public disapproval of Hartford Convention lead to demise of Federalist party
   4. 1816, Republican James Monroe wins presidency against minimal Federalist opposition; carries every electoral vote but one in election of 1820

IV. The Awakening of U.S. Nationalism
  A. *Madison's Nationalism and the Era of Good Feelings*
   1. Postwar period (Era of Good Feelings) characterized by heightened nationalism, new political consensus
   2. Republicans embrace some Federalist ideas: charter new national bank and pass protective tariff, but Madison vetoes internal improvements bill, 1817
   3. Henry Clay advocates American System: national bank, federal aid for internal improvements, protective tariff to encourage domestic manufacturing
   4. Sectional harmony starts to break down over issue of slavery and its spread westward
  B. *John Marshall and the Supreme Court*
   1. *Dartmouth College* v. *Woodward* (1819) limits state power to interfere with contracts and charters
   2. *McCulloch* v. *Maryland* (1819) upholds broad interpretation of Constitution and implied powers of federal government
   3. Republicans dislike *Dartmouth* and *McCulloch* decisions because they prevent states from exercising authority over corporations and give too much power to federal government
  C. *The Missouri Compromise*

Jeffersonianism and the Era of Good Feelings

1. Missouri controversy involves issues of slavery, sectionalism, party politics
2. 1820, Congress approves Missouri Compromise: Missouri enters the Union as a slave state; Maine enters as a free state; in remainder of Louisiana Territory, slavery permitted only south of 36°30′ latitude
3. Compromise bans slavery from most of Midwest and West, reinforces principle that Congress can prohibit slavery in territories, keeps even balance of free and slave states

D. Foreign Policy under Monroe
1. 1816–1824, Secretary of State John Quincy Adams shapes U.S. foreign policy
2. Rush-Bagot Treaty (1817) and British-American Convention (1818) cement good relations between United States and British-owned Canada; set U.S.-Canadian border
3. Andrew Jackson raids Florida, 1818
4. Adams uses raid to pressure Spain into signing Adams-Onís (Transcontinental) Treaty; Spain cedes East Florida to the United States, renounces claims to West Florida

E. The Monroe Doctrine
1. Spain attempts to regain its Latin American empire
2. British propose joint U.S.-British statement opposing attempts by Spain and its allies to interfere in South America
3. Adams and Monroe prefer separate U.S. statement; issue the Monroe Doctrine: United States will not become involved in strictly European affairs, the American continents are not available for further European colonization, the United States looks upon any attempt by European countries to regain lost colonies or to interfere in Americas as an unfriendly act
4. Importance of Monroe Doctrine: becomes cornerstone of U.S. foreign policy, keeps open U.S. options to expand in Latin America, claims United States has preeminent position in Western Hemisphere

Vocabulary

The following terms are used in Chapter 8. To understand the chapter fully, it is important that you know what each of them means.

infidel an unbeliever; one who does not accept a particular religion, such as Christianity

nonpartisan not influenced by political party bias or affiliation

judicial review right of the federal courts to declare legislative acts unconstitutional

impeach to charge a public official, such as a judge or president, with misconduct in office. An impeachment means an indictment, not a conviction, and a trial must follow unless the impeached official resigns

coalition a combination or alliance among different groups, parties, or states in support of a particular cause, individual, or purpose

internal improvements roads, canals, and other projects to improve transportation and communication

consensus general agreement

Identifications

After reading Chapter 8, you should be able to identify and explain the historical significance of each of the following:

Tripolitan (Barbary) pirates
Judiciary Act of 1801
midnight judges
Marbury v. *Madison*
John Marshall
Lewis and Clark expedition
Sacajawea
Aaron Burr conspiracy
impressment
Chesapeake-Leopard Affair
Embargo and Non-Intercourse Acts
war hawks
Tecumseh and the Prophet
William Henry Harrison and the battles of Tippecanoe and the Thames
Oliver H. Perry and the Battle of Lake Erie
Treaty of Ghent and the *status quo antebellum*
Battle of New Orleans
Hartford Convention
Henry Clay and the American System
Era of Good Feelings
Dartmouth College v. *Woodward*
McCulloch v. *Maryland*
Missouri Compromise
John Quincy Adams
Rush-Bagot Treaty and British-American Convention
Adams-Onís (Transcontinental) Treaty
Monroe Doctrine

Skill Building: Maps

On the map of the United States, locate each of the places listed below. How is each connected with one or more of the following historical events: U.S. treaties with Spain and France, the Lewis and Clark expedition, the War of 1812, and sectional conflict and compromise?

East and West Florida

New Orleans

Louisiana Territory

Appalachian Mountains

Mississippi River

Missouri River

Snake River

Columbia River

St. Louis

Ohio River

Lake Erie, Lake Ontario, and Lake Champlain

Chesapeake Bay

36°30′ latitude

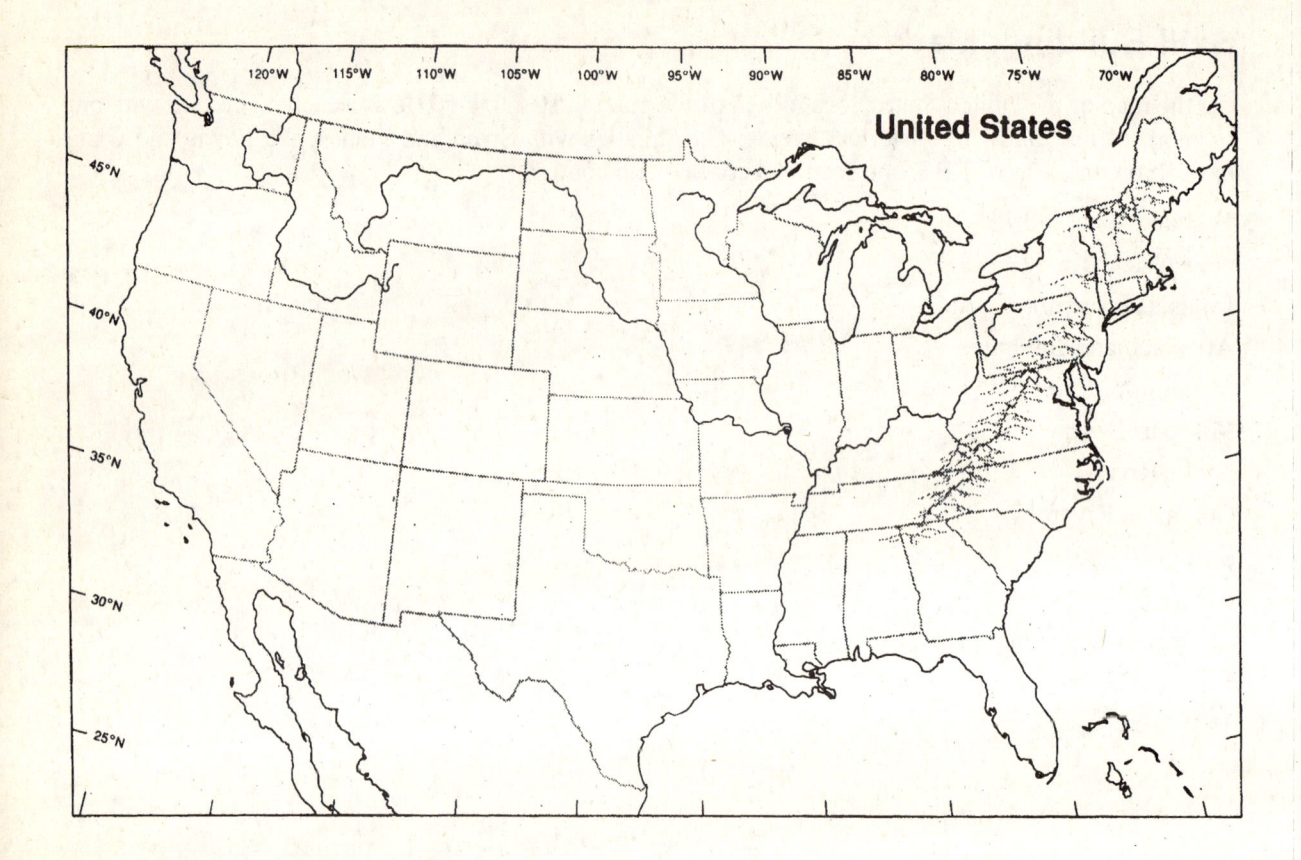

Multiple-Choice Questions

Circle the letter of the item that best completes each statement or answers the question.

1. Between 1800 and 1823, the United States did all the following *except*
    a. fight a war it almost lost.
    b. extend the right to vote to women and blacks.
    c. double in territorial size.
    d. warn European powers not to claim new colonies in the Americas.

2. Thomas Jefferson believed that
    a. educated farmers were the most virtuous citizens and best upholders of republican liberty.
    b. state governments had too much power and the federal government had not enough.
    c. the United States should develop prosperous cities, filled with new industries.
    d. the rich should pay heavier taxes so that government could provide more social services for the poor.

3. Chief Justice John Marshall's opinions backed which of the following?
   a. the right of federal courts to declare acts of Congress unconstitutional
   b. a broad definition of treason that made convicting the accused easier
   c. a narrow interpretation of the Constitution, which denied that the federal government had any powers beyond those enumerated in the document
   d. the doctrine that states could nullify actions of the federal government

4. The Embargo Act
   a. badly damaged the British economy.
   b. stimulated the growth of manufacturing in the United States.
   c. induced the French to drop their trade restrictions against the United States.
   d. was favored in New England but resisted in the South.

5. Thomas Jefferson briefly hesitated accepting Napoleon's offer to sell the Louisiana Territory to the United States because
   a. he doubted that it was worth Napoleon's $15 million asking price.
   b. he knew that much of the territory was a desert, unsuitable for agriculture.
   c. he believed in strict interpretation of the Constitution and wanted to wait for ratification of an amendment authorizing land purchase.
   d. he did not want to unbalance the federal budget.

6. By the terms of the Ghent Treaty, which ended the War of 1812,
   a. the United States gained Florida and some territory from Canada.
   b. the British agreed to stop impressment and other violations of U.S. neutral rights.
   c. neither the United States nor Great Britain gained territory or made concessions.
   d. the British agreed to evacuate New Orleans and to compensate the United States for burning Washington.

7. The war hawks were
   a. mostly from New England.
   b. eager for war against Napoleon to gain the Louisiana Territory.
   c. supporters of Thomas Jefferson's and James Madison's policy of economic coercion.
   d. Republicans from the West and South who wanted to take Canada from Great Britain and Florida from Spain.

8. Which one of the following provisions was *not* a part of the Missouri Compromise?
   a. All children of Missouri slaves born after Missouri became a state would be emancipated at age twenty-five.
   b. Maine was admitted to the Union as a free state.
   c. Slavery would be barred from the Louisiana Territory north of 36°30′ latitude, except for Missouri.
   d. Missouri was admitted as a slave state.

9. Secretary of State John Quincy Adams is associated with which of the following foreign-policy initiatives?
   a. purchasing Texas from Mexico
   b. purchasing Louisiana
   c. formulating the Monroe Doctrine and purchasing Florida
   d. British sale of the Oregon Territory to the United States for $15 million

10. During the Era of Good Feelings,
    a. the Federalist party disappeared, but the Republican party adopted some of its policies.
    b. the United States won a war against England.
    c. sectional and partisan conflicts became more acute.
    d. President James Monroe signed treaties of alliance with Great Britain and France.

11. During the War of 1812,
    a. the United States successfully occupied Canada.
    b. the British captured Baltimore, Maryland.
    c. Tecumseh, the Prophet, and their Native American followers proved valuable allies to the Americans against the British.
    d. the northeastern states became increasingly unhappy about the war.

12. Which of the following sequences of events is in the correct chronological order?
    a. The Era of Good Feelings, James Madison's first election as president, the Embargo Act, *Marbury* v. *Madison*
    b. James Monroe's first election as president, *Marbury* v. *Madison*, the Hartford Convention, end of the Federalist party
    c. resumption of the Napoleonic wars in Europe, the Hartford Convention, Thomas Jefferson's first election as president, the War of 1812
    d. Thomas Jefferson's first election as president, the Louisiana Purchase, James Madison's first election as president, Congress's declaration of war on Great Britain

Essay Questions

1. Compare and contrast the political and economic views of the Hamiltonian Federalists and the Jeffersonian Republicans. When, why, and how did the differences between the two parties blur?

2. Thomas Jefferson's first term as president was so successful that he overwhelmingly won reelection in 1804. His second term, in contrast, was marked by frustration and failure. Discuss the achievements of Jefferson's first term and the problems that beset his second.

3. Discuss the foreign-policy achievements of President James Monroe and his secretary of state, John Quincy Adams. How do those achievements still affect the United States and its foreign policy today?

Jeffersonianism and the Era of Good Feelings 101

4. Why did the United States engage in a nearly disastrous war against Great Britain from 1812 to 1814? What, if anything, did the United States gain from that war? What political consequences did the war have?

5. Your textbook says of the Era of Good Feelings that followed the War of 1812 that "the good feelings were paper-thin" and the "postwar consensus unraveled rapidly." Write an essay discussing the reasons for the brief political consensus and pointing to legislative signs of it. Then explain why the political harmony was "paper-thin" and "unraveled rapidly." What were the political signs of the unraveling?

Answers to Multiple-Choice Questions

1a. No. The U.S. did fight a war it almost lost: the War of 1812.
1b. Yes. That was something the United States did not do between 1800 and 1823.
1c. No. The United States did double its size with the Louisiana Purchase.
1d. No. The United States did issue such a warning in the Monroe Doctrine, 1823.

2a. Yes. See page 151.
2b. No. Jefferson believed just the opposite.
2c. No. Jefferson feared cities and the propertyless mobs that could form in them.
2d. No. Jefferson believed taxes should be kept minimal and government should take on very limited responsibilities.

3a. Yes. In *Marbury* v. *Madison*. See page 154.
3b. No. Marshall showed he opposed a broad definition of treason in the way he handled the case against Aaron Burr.
3c. No. Marshall claimed just the opposite in *McCulloch* v. *Maryland*.
3d. No. Marshall's decisions pointed to the supremacy of federal law over state.

4a. No. The British got needed food from Canada and other sources.
4b. Yes. Merchants, unable to make money in shipping, invested their capital in new mills.
4c. No. They did not.
4d. No. The Embargo was especially hated in New England, which lived by import-export and shipping.

5a. No. $15,000,000 was a bargain.
5b. No. Not true and he didn't know that.
5c. Yes. See page 156.
5d. No. Jefferson knew it was worth spending the money to make our border secure, gain control of New Orleans and the mouth of the Mississippi, and double the size of our country.

6a. No. Not in Treaty of Ghent.
6b. No. They made no concessions on impressment.
6c. Yes. See page 164.
6d. No. Not in Treaty of Ghent.

7a. No. New England was making money shipping to Britain and France despite the interference with our trade, and they feared war would ruin this lucrative trade.
7b. No. The United States had already bought the Louisiana Territory.
7c. No. They were impatient with Jefferson's and Madison's policy of economic coercion, which didn't work.
7d. Yes. See page 160.

Copyright © Houghton Mifflin Company. All rights reserved.

Chapter 8

8a. Yes. This provision was dropped from the Compromise. See pages 166-167.
8b. No. This was a part of the Compromise.
8c. No. See 8b.
8d. No. See 8b.

9a. No. Texas was acquired in the 1840s, touching off the Mexican War.
9b. No. Accomplished during Jefferson's presidency, in 1803.
9c. Yes. See page 168.
9d. No. Not how the United States acquired Oregon and it happened in the late 1840s

10a. Yes. See page 165.
10b. No. The Era of Good Feelings followed the War of 1812, which the United States almost lost.
10c. No. For a short while they seemed to calm down, though they were just below the surface and would soon reemerge.
10d. No. The United States avoided signing alliances with European countries.

11a. No. All U. S. attempts were driven back.
11b. No. They tried to but failed.
11c. No. Tecumseh and his followers allied with the British.
11d. Yes. See pages 164-165.

12a. No. The correct dates are: Marbury v. Madison (1803), the Embargo Act (1807), Madison's first election (1808), Era of Good Feelings (1814-1820).
12b. No. The correct dates are: *Marbury* v. *Madison* (1803), Hartford Convention (1814), Monroe elected (1816), end of Federalist party (1814-1816).
12c. No. The correct dates are: Jefferson's first election (1800), resumption of Napoleonic wars (1803), War of 1812 (1812-1814), Hartford Convention (1814).
12d. Yes. Jefferson's first election (1800), Louisiana Purchase (1803), Madison's election (1808), Congress declares war on Great Britain (1812).

CHAPTER 9

The Transformation of American Society, 1815–1840

Outline

I. **Westward Expansion and the Growth of the Market Economy**
   A. *The Sweep West*
      1. Stages of westward movement: by 1803 Vermont, Kentucky, Tennessee, Ohio become states; by 1821 Indiana, Mississippi, Illinois, Alabama, Maine, Missouri enter the Union
      2. Jedediah Smith and the "mountain men" roam beyond Rockies
      3. Typical westward migrants settle between the Appalachian Mountains and the Mississippi River
   B. *Western Society and Customs*
      1. Migration of families predominates
      2. Settlement along navigable rivers with others from the same region
      3. Before 1830 life in West crude, difficult; easterners look down on westerners' lack of refinement; westerners resent eastern pretensions to gentility
   C. *The Federal Government and the West*
      1. Federal government actions, treaties, and policies that encourage westward expansion of whites: Ordinance of 1785, Northwest Ordinance (1787), Louisiana Purchase (1803), Adams-Onís Treaty (1819), land warrants given to War of 1812 veterans, extension of National Road to Illinois (1838)
      2. Louisiana Purchase, Adams-Onís Treaty, War of 1812 strip Native Americans of Spanish and British protection
   D. *The Removal of Native Americans*
      1. The "Five Civilized Tribes" live in the Southeast
      2. Indian Removal Act of 1830 grants president authority to remove tribes by force; Andrew Jackson happily enforces the law
      3. Creeks, Chickasaws, Choctaws, and Seminoles in 1830s and 1840s forced to relocate
      4. *Worcester* v. *Georgia* (1832): Chief Justice John Marshall rules the Cherokees have right to remain on their lands in Georgia; President Jackson disregards decision; forces tribe west on Trail of Tears

5. Indians lose Black Hawk War and the Sac and Fox tribes removed (1830s)
E. *The Agricultural Boom*
1. Western settlement stimulated by Native American removal and price boom in agricultural commodities
2. Reasons for growing commodity demand and rising prices: British textile industry demand for raw cotton; European and New England need for foodstuffs
F. *The Market Economy and Federal Land Policy*
1. Change from subsistence farming to commercial farming
2. Debt and other economic problems burden commercial farmers
3. Evolution of federal land policy: easier for small farmers to buy, 1800–1820 government cuts minimum acres that can be purchased
4. Land speculators, using easy credit, often acquire best land at public auctions
G. *The Speculator and the Squatter*
1. Squatters hate speculators
2. Squatters press for "preemption" rights over speculators, which they win in 1841
3. Farmers caught in debt
H. *The Panic of 1819*
1. Western land boom collapses in the Panic of 1819
2. Causes: overdependence on foreign markets; overextension of credit; national bank tightens credit, calls in notes of western banks, many of which subsequently fail
3. Consequences: frontier hatred of banks (especially Bank of the United States), demand for protective tariffs and internal improvements
I. *The Transportation Revolution: Steamboats, Canals, and Railroads*
1. Weaknesses of the pre-1820 transportation system: existing roads and turnpikes inadequate for moving bulky products, too expensive and slow
2. Robert Livingston, Robert Fulton, and their steamship the *Clermont* (1807); *Gibbons* v. *Ogden* breaks their transportation monopoly and upholds national authority in interstate commerce over state interference, steamboat travel increases
3. Steamboats ply the Mississippi and Ohio Rivers
4. Canal-building boom follows successful completion of Erie Canal (1825)
5. Growth of railroads; 1840 total railroad-track mileage equals total canal mileage
6. Advantages and disadvantages of railroads compared with canals: railroads cheaper to build, can reach more places; canals built with help of state taxes (railroads have to depend on private capital), need little maintenance, cheaper for shipping bulky goods than rail
J. *The Growth of Cities*
1. The transportation revolution stimulates the growth of cities; 1820–1860, period of fastest urbanization in U.S. history
2. Urban growth particularly fast in the West
3. Industrialization also spurs urbanization

II. The Rise of Manufacturing

A. Causes of Industrialization
1. Protective tariffs shield domestic manufacturers from foreign competition
2. Transportation revolution enlarges markets and demand
3. Immigration: British bring technological know-how; Irish and Germans provide labor and customers
4. Scarcity and costliness of labor in early United States encourage new labor-saving machines and techniques
5. Eli Whitney introduces interchangeable parts, comes to be known as the American System of manufacturing

B. The Faces of Industrialization
1. Reasons for New England's industrializing first: disruption of its foreign trade (1808–1815) leads merchants to shift capital to manufacturing; swift-flowing rivers for waterpower; excess female farm population for labor
2. Samuel Slater opens mill in Rhode Island (1790)
3. The Boston Manufacturing Company (1813) builds mills at Lowell and Waltham
4. Lowell and Waltham mills concentrate total cloth production in factory; at first, 80 percent of employees are unmarried women, supervised by hired managers, disciplined by company rules; 1830s, pay decreases, worsening conditions lead many native-born farm women to quit
5. New York City and Philadelphia manufacturing use fewer machines, more manual labor than New England mills; piece work brought to homes of widows, immigrants, and other cheap laborers; skilled artisans hurt
6. To protect themselves, skilled workers found trade unions, workingmen's political parties; skilled and unskilled workers stage strikes

III. Equality and Inequality

A. Growing Inequality: The Rich and the Poor
1. Widening gap between rich and poor
2. Greater inequality in cities than countryside
3. The "rags to riches" myth not borne out: fewer than 5 percent of well-to-do start out poor
4. Urban rich build splendid houses, join exclusive clubs
5. Urban poor live close to subsistence, depend on wages of children to supplement family income, are periodically unemployed
6. Pauperism and who fell into it: ill, widowed, Irish immigrants fleeing famine, northern free blacks
7. Attitudes about the poor: U.S. tendency to blame poor for their condition

B. Free Blacks in the North
1. Victims of prejudice and discrimination

Chapter 9

  2. Have limited economic opportunities, are segregated from whites, usually denied right to vote
 C. The "Middling Classes"
  1. Majority of Americans in middling classes
  2. Middling classes after 1800 have rising income and standard of living
  3. Middling classes have new economic opportunities but also greater insecurity
  4. Both poor and middling classes must move frequently to make a living

IV. **The Revolution in Social Relationships**
 A. *Introduction*
  1. Economic change affects traditional social relationships
  2. Authority questioned; deference declines after War of 1812
  3. Forging new foundations for authority and founding new voluntary organizations
 B. *The Attack on the Professions*
  1. Criticism of professionals; erosion of traditional authority
  2. Belief spreads that doctors, lawyers, other professionals need no special education or license
  3. Questioning of traditional authority figures most pronounced on the frontier
 C. *The Challenges to Family Authority*
  1. Loosening of parental authority: young men leave home at early age, strike out on their own
  2. Changing courtship and marriage patterns: young people increasingly make own choice of whom to marry or even whether to marry
 D. *Wives, Husbands*
  1. Relationships between spouses changing
  2. Idea of "separate spheres" for men and women gaining acceptance as alternative to legal equality for wife
  3. White middle-class women gain more control over size of their families; birthrate for them drops; birthrates remain high among blacks, immigrants, and in rural West
 E. *Horizontal Allegiances and the Rise of Voluntary Associations*
  1. Substitution of horizontal allegiances for vertical allegiances
  2. Voluntary associations proliferate in the 1820s and 1830s; temperance and moral reform societies of white middle-class women and black voluntary associations attempt to increase members' influence in society

Vocabulary

The following terms are used in Chapter 9. To understand the chapter fully, it is important that you know what each of them means.

public domain the land owned by the government

subsistence farming growing crops to feed and satisfy a farm family's own needs rather than to sell on the market

commercial farming growing crops for sale on the market; farming as a business, big or small

squatter one who settles on land, especially public or new land, without title or right

preemption the act or right of purchasing before others or in preference to others

specie gold, silver, or other coined money (as opposed to paper currency)

capital wealth (money) used or capable of being used in the production of more wealth

technology the industrial arts; technical advances in production methods

antebellum before the war; pre–Civil War

myth a collective belief that is built up in response to the wishes of the group rather than with a basis in fact

pauperism the condition of being without means of support and living on public or private charity

transient one who moves frequently from place to place (as opposed to establishing permanent residence over long periods)

proliferation rapid growth or increase in number

Identifications

After reading Chapter 9, you should be able to identify and explain the historical significance of each of the following:

John Jacob Astor

"mountain men": Kit Carson and Jedediah Smith

"Five Civilized Tribes"

Indian Removal Act, 1830

Worcester v. *Georgia*

Trail of Tears

Black Hawk War

transportation revolution

Panic of 1819

Robert Livingston, Robert Fulton, the *Clermont,* and the Livingston-Fulton monopoly

Gibbons v. *Ogden*

Erie Canal

Samuel Slater

Eli Whitney and interchangeable parts

"cottage" manufacturing

Boston Manufacturing Company, the Waltham and Lowell mills

Copyright © Houghton Mifflin Company. All rights reserved.

Alexis de Tocqueville, *Democracy in America*

middling classes

Multiple-Choice Questions

Circle the letter of the item that best completes each statement or answers the question.

1. Andrew Jackson's remark, "John Marshall has made his decision; now let him enforce it," refers to the president's intention to
   a. destroy the national bank despite the Supreme Court ruling upholding its constitutionality.
   b. use force, if necessary, to make South Carolina obey federal laws that it thought unconstitutional.
   c. move the Cherokees west of the Mississippi, regardless of Supreme Court rulings.
   d. disregard Chief Justice Marshall's ruling in *Gibbons* v. *Ogden*.

2. All of the following statements about the National Road are correct *except*
   a. it became one of the major routes used by families migrating from the mid-Atlantic states to the Midwest.
   b. it stretched as far west as Illinois by 1840.
   c. it was one of the few internal improvements financed by federal tax money before the Civil War.
   d. it was built by a private company that charged travelers tolls for using it.

3. By 1840 approximately what proportion of Americans lived between the Appalachian Mountains and the Mississippi River?
   a. one-fourth
   b. one-third
   c. one-half
   d. two-thirds

4. Which of the following was most responsible for the spread of cotton growing into the Old Southwest?
   a. the discovery of methods for getting sea-island cotton to flourish in the interior uplands
   b. the removal of the "Five Civilized Tribes"
   c. the adoption of a homestead law making the available land free to qualified settlers
   d. Eli Whitney's invention of the cotton gin

5. Which of the following statements about the Erie Canal is correct?
   a. It linked New York City through inland waterways to Ohio and made the city a major outlet for midwestern produce.
   b. It and the National Road were the only major internal improvements financed by the federal government before the Civil War.
   c. It contributed to the growing importance of Mississippi River cities such as New Orleans.
   d. It had little impact on shipping costs.

6. The Panic of 1819 resulted in which of the following?
   a. getting western farmers to return to subsistence farming
   b. making many westerners hate the national bank
   c. making westerners reluctant to see federal tax monies spent on expensive internal improvements
   d. making industrialists denounce high U.S. tariffs for ruining their sales abroad

7. In the 1820s and 1830s the majority of the workers in the Lowell and Waltham textile mills were
   a. children from poor immigrant families.
   b. Irish and French-Canadian immigrants.
   c. displaced artisans and skilled workers.
   d. young women from New England farms.

8. Which of the following statements about the professions in the late 1840s is correct?
   a. Lawyers, doctors, and clergymen were highly paid and respected.
   b. Women were entering the professions in significant numbers.
   c. No state required a person to have medical education or a license to be a doctor.
   d. Increasing numbers of doctors, lawyers, and ministers moved to the West because they were most needed and valued there.

9. By the mid-1830s which of the following accounted for two-thirds of U.S. foreign exports?
   a. wheat and corn
   b. textiles
   c. cotton
   d. farm machinery

10. The transportation revolution in the years after the War of 1812 contributed to the growth of which of the following?
    a. commercial farming in the West
    b. industry in the Deep South
    c. new markets for southeastern cotton growers in the West
    d. more diversified agriculture in the South

11. The majority of the immigrants who arrived in the United States in the 1840s and 1850s were from
    a. England and Scotland.
    b. Italy and Eastern Europe.
    c. Ireland and Germany.
    d. Asia and Latin America.

110   Chapter 9

12. Which of the following statements about the U.S. class structure between 1815 and 1840 is correct?
    a. The United States had virtually no pauperized class.
    b. The majority of Americans belonged to the middling classes.
    c. The majority of the wealthy had started out in the working class and had then made fortunes out of industrial expansion or land speculation.
    d. The gap between the rich and the poor was greater in the country than in the cities.

Essay Questions

1. Discuss the idea of separate spheres for women. In what ways did the idea serve to empower women? In what ways was it a substitute for real equality between men and women?

2. Discuss the transportation revolution between 1815 and 1840. What changes took place? What was the impact of those changes on the nation economically, politically, and socially?

3. Alexis de Tocqueville, in his *Democracy in America,* was impressed by the "general equality of condition among the people." Writing about the same period, New York merchant Philip Hone stated "the two extremes of costly luxury in living, expensive establishments, and improvident waste are presented in daily and hourly contrast with squalid misery and hopeless destitution." How do you account for these very different assessments? Which man came closer to the truth? Why?

4. Discuss federal government policy toward Native Americans between 1815 and 1840.

5. Your textbook states that "the antebellum era witnessed the widespread substitution of *horizontal* allegiances for *vertical* allegiances." What does this mean, and what evidence does the chapter offer to support the claim?

Answers to Multiple-Choice Questions

1a. No. Jackson did decide to destroy the national bank, but did not make the remark in that connection.
1b. No. Jackson did decide to make South Carolina obey federal law, but did not make the remark in that connection.
1c. Yes. See page 174.
1d. No. Jackson did not disregard the *Gibbons* v. *Ogden* decision.

2a. No. This statement is correct.
2b. No. This statement is correct.
2c. No. This statement is correct.
2d. Yes. This statement is incorrect because the Federal government built it and did not charge tolls. See page 173.

3a. No. It was greater than one-fourth.
3b. Yes. See page 171.
3c. No. It was less than one-half.
3d. No. Figure much too high.

Copyright © Houghton Mifflin Company. All rights reserved.

4a. No. That never happened.
4b. No. That opened new lands for white farmers, but was not the most responsible.
4c. No. That did not happen until 1862.
4d. Yes. See page 175.

5a. Yes. See page 177.
5b. No. The building of the Erie Canal was financed by the State of New York.
5c. No. It had just the opposite effect. The importance of Mississippi River ports declined.
5d. No. It had dramatic impact on shipping costs, greatly reducing them.

6a. No. That didn't happen.
6b. Yes. See pages 176-177.
6c. No. Just the opposite, westerners realized how badly they needed good transportation to reach distant markets.
6d. No. U.S. industrialists generally favored high protective tariffs to keep cheaper manufactured goods from Europe out of the American market.

7a. No. Not in the 1820s and 1830s.
7b. No. That would not be the case until the 1840s and 1850s.
7c. No. Mostly unskilled labor was needed in the textile mills.
7d. Yes. See page 179.

8a. No. They were increasingly criticized and often received little respect.
8b. No. That would not happen for many years to come.
8c. Yes. See page 182.
8d. No. They may have been needed there, but they received the least respect on the frontier.

9a. No. They were important but not the main export.
9b. No. Our textile industry was not yet that developed.
9c. Yes. See page 175.
9d. No. The United States had almost no farm machinery manufacturing yet.

10a. Yes. See page 175.
10b. No. There was almost none.
10c. No. Because there were few textile mills in the West.
10d. No. Increasingly the South concentrated on growing cotton.

11a. No. That was in the colonial period.
11b. No. That became true only after 1880.
11c. Yes. See page 178.
11d. No. That did not become true until after 1965.

12a. No. In the cities that group was growing.
12b. Yes. See page 181.
12c. No. That was the myth, but it was never the reality.
12d. No. Just the opposite was true.

Copyright © Houghton Mifflin Company. All rights reserved.

CHAPTER 10
Politics, Religion, and Reform in Antebellum America

Outline

I. **The Transformation of U.S. Politics, 1824–1832**

   A. *Introduction*
   1. Reasons for split of Republican party: tensions over industrialization, slavery, westward expansion
   2. Democrats and states' rights versus Whigs and federally encouraged economic development
   3. Politics as expression of the common people's will

   B. *Democratic Ferment*
   1. The political parties court voters; politics democratize
   2. End of property qualification for voting
   3. Use of written ballots
   4. Shift from appointive to elective offices
   5. Popular election of members of electoral college

   C. *The Election of 1824*
   1. Impact of sectionalism; four Republican candidates for president: John Quincy Adams, Andrew Jackson, William Crawford, Henry Clay
   2. Jackson wins popular vote, not electoral college majority
   3. Clay backs Adams; House of Representatives names Adams president
   4. Adams appoints Clay secretary of state; Jackson supporters claim "corrupt bargain" between Adams and Clay

   D. *John Quincy Adams as President*
   1. Adams for federally financed internal improvements; old-line Republicans against
   2. Adams offends proslavery southerners
   3. Adams poor politician

   E. *The Rise of Andrew Jackson*
   1. Jackson's growing popularity stemming from voter disaffection for Adams,

Politics, Religion, and Reform in Antebellum America   113

        Jackson's military heroism, southern approval of Jackson's slaveholding and policies toward Native Americans, Jackson's lack of association with Panic of 1819
      2. Rise of Martin Van Buren as new breed of politician and organizer of Democratic party
      3. Second party system emerging: Democrats against National Republicans
  F. *The Election of 1828*
      1. Nasty, mudslinging campaign
      2. Candidates for president: Jackson (Democrat) versus Adams (National Republican)
      3. Jackson wins with heaviest support from South and Southwest
  G. *Jackson in Office*
      1. Jackson uses and defends the spoils system
      2. Jackson's opposition to federal aid for internal improvements; Maysville Road Bill veto pleases the South
      3. Southerners blame Jackson for Tariff of 1828
  H. *Nullification*
      1. "Tariff of Abominations" (1828) hated by South; produces split between Jackson and Vice President John C. Calhoun
      2. Calhoun's *South Carolina Exposition and Protest* (1828): protective tariff unconstitutional, therefore states have right to nullify it
  I. *Jackson versus Calhoun*
      1. Jackson's attempts to placate South: returns surplus tariff revenue to the states, backs slightly lower tariff of 1832
      2. Calhoun and South Carolina not satisfied
      3. Other tensions between Jackson and Calhoun: Jackson's unauthorized Florida raid; the Peggy Eaton affair
      4. South Carolina nullifies tariffs of 1828 and 1832
      5. Jackson denounces nullification; signs Compromise Tariff of 1833 and Force Bill
      6. Henry Clay's Compromise of 1833: tariff rates lowered, South Carolina nullification rescinded
  J. *The Bank Veto*
      1. Jackson suspicious of banks, paper money, monopolies
      2. Jackson's and Democrats' hatred of the Bank of the United States: blame it for Panic of 1819, consider it privileged monopoly, dislike its control by "monied capitalists," view it harmful to economic interests of West
      3. Bank president Nicholas Biddle applies for recharter
      4. Jackson vetoes Clay's recharter bill (1832)
  K. *The Election of 1832*
      1. Jackson defends both states' rights and indivisibility of the Union
      2. Jackson (Democrat) versus Clay (National Republican)

Copyright © Houghton Mifflin Company. All rights reserved.

3. Clay runs on the American System: protective tariff, national bank, federally supported internal improvements
4. Jackson wins, plans to complete destruction of Bank of the United States

II. The Bank Controversy and the Second Party System

A. The War on the Bank of the United States
   1. Jackson removes federal funds from Bank of the United States, and deposits them in state banks ("pet banks")
   2. Federal monies in state banks fuel credit expansion, speculation, inflation

B. The Rise of Whig Opposition
   1. Conversion of National Republicans to Whigs
   2. Whig supporters: southerners offended by Jackson's nullification stand, defenders of Bank of the United States and federally funded internal improvements, believers in more federal government intervention, northern reformers, Anti-Masons
   3. Whigs a national party by 1836; united by opposition to Jackson

C. The Election of 1836
   1. Whigs run four candidates for president; Democrats charge they hope to throw election into House of Representatives
   2. Democrats nominate Van Buren
   3. Van Buren wins narrow victory

D. The Panic of 1837
   1. Van Buren inherits Panic of 1837 and depression
   2. Causes of depression: Jackson's bank war, pet banks, and Specie Circular (1836); British cutoff of specie to United States

E. The Search for Solutions
   1. Van Buren signs the Independent Treasury Bill: federal funds deposited in government vaults, not banks
   2. Whigs blame depression on Jackson's Specie Circular; favor bank notes and credit
   3. Democrats blame banks and speculation for depression; oppose banks and bank notes

F. The Election of 1840
   1. Van Buren (Democrat) versus William Henry Harrison (Whig)
   2. Whigs adopt no platform, use campaign symbols and slogans: log cabin, "Tippecanoe and Tyler too!"
   3. Harrison wins

G. The Second Party System Matures
   1. Heavy voter turnout in 1840
   2. Causes of big turnout: depression, colorful campaigning
   3. High voter interest sustained by hardening party differences after 1840

III. The Rise of Popular Religion

A. The Second Great Awakening

Copyright © Houghton Mifflin Company. All rights reserved.

1. 1790–1840s, series of emotional religious revivals
2. Revivalism spreads from New England to western frontier
3. Methodists become largest Protestant denomination; use itinerant circuit riders in the West

B. *Eastern Revivals*
   1. Shift of Great Awakening to western New York, "Burned-Over District" (1820s)
   2. Charles G. Finney's preaching: rejection of Calvinist predestination; affirmation of human ability to reject sin; necessity of emotional religious conversion
   3. Reasons for Finney's appeal: democratizing of religious doctrine, asserting of individual's control over his destiny, reaching out to women

C. *Critics of Revivals: The Unitarians*
   1. Unitarians have doubts about revivals: they stress long-term character building over sudden emotional conversion
   2. Unitarianism appeals to wealthy and educated
   3. Both Unitarians and revivalists reject Calvinist view of human depravity

D. *The Rise of Mormonism*
   1. Joseph Smith founds Church of Jesus Christ of Latter-Day Saints (Mormonism), 1820s
   2. Mormons start to practice polygyny
   3. Mormons persecuted, Smith murdered
   4. Brigham Young leads Mormons to Utah

E. *The Shakers*
   1. Mother Ann Lee, founder of the Shakers (1770s)
   2. Shakers establish communities of handicrafts and farming
   3. Shakers and Mormons withdraw from society
   4. Majority of Evangelicals active in society and reform efforts

IV. **The Age of Reform**

A. *Introduction*
   1. Growth of membership in social-reform organizations in 1820s and 1830s
   2. Reform movements strongest in New England and parts of Midwest settled by New Englanders

B. *The War on Liquor*
   1. Problem of alcohol abuse
   2. Lyman Beecher establishes the American Temperance Society (1825)
   3. Supporters of temperance reform: women, employers
   4. Workers form Washington Temperance Societies (1840)
   5. Reduced alcohol consumption by the 1840s

C. *Public-School Reform*
   1. Horace Mann's reforms: state tax support of schools, compulsory attendance, longer

school term, standardized textbooks, students separated into grades
		2. Goals of reformers: spread uniform cultural values, combat ignorance, teach discipline, prepare work force for industrializing capitalist economy, assimilate immigrants, inculcate patriotism
		3. Supporters of school reform: northerners, urban workers, manufacturers, women, native born
		4. Opponents: some farmers, Catholics, working poor
		5. Blacks and whites segregated in schools
	D. Abolitionism
		1. American Colonization Society (1817): gradual compensated emancipation, return of blacks to Africa
		2. More radical black antislavery views; David Walker; no forced return to Africa
		3. William Lloyd Garrison, *The Liberator* (1831); immediate emancipation, equal rights for blacks; supported by African-Americans
		4. Frederick Douglass, leading African-American abolitionist
		5. American Anti-Slavery Society (1833): internal divisions over forming political party and women's rights
		6. Congress, annoyed by antislavery petitions, passes the "gag rule"; John Quincy Adams fights for freedom of petition; "gag rule" repealed, 1845
	E. Women's Rights
		1. Women reformers in abolitionist movement: Angelina and Sarah Grimké, Lucretia Mott, Lucy Stone, Abby Kelley
		2. Discrimination against women abolitionists at World Anti-Slavery Convention leads to Mott's and Elizabeth Cady Stanton's call to Seneca Falls women's rights convention, 1848
		3. "Declaration of Sentiments" and resolutions issued by the convention
		4. Reasons for slow progress of women's rights reform: satisfaction with partial victories, "cult of domesticity"
	F. Penitentiaries and Asylums
		1. Reformers' views on causes of poverty, crime, insanity: lack of proper moral influences
		2. Reformers' remedy: create regimented institutions to impose moral discipline
		3. Penitentiaries: "Auburn system" and "Pennsylvania system"
		4. Almshouses and workhouses for the indigent
		5. Dorothea Dix convinces many states to establish insane asylums
	G. Utopian Communities
		1. Attempts to form cooperative communities as alternatives to competitive, materialistic capitalism
		2. Robert Owen and New Harmony (1820s)
		3. Brook Farm, transcendentalists, *The Dial*
		4. John Humphrey Noyes and Oneida

Vocabulary

The following terms are used in Chapter 10. To understand the chapter fully, it is important that you know what each of them means.

suffrage the vote; the right to vote

nullify to render or declare legally void or inoperative

itinerant traveling from place to place

proselytizer person who seeks to make new converts

utopian founded upon or involving perfection in law, politics, and human relations

deviancy behavior differing from the normal, accepted behavior and/or morality of the society

evangelical Protestantism forms of Protestantism that stress the importance of experiencing an emotional religious conversion

Identifications

After reading Chapter 10, you should be able to identify and explain the historical significance of each of the following:

Henry Clay and the American System

second American party system

spoils system

Tariff of Abominations, 1828

John C. Calhoun and the *South Carolina Exposition and Protest*

Compromise of 1833

Nicholas Biddle and the Bank of the United States

Specie Circular

Log Cabin campaign, "Tippecanoe and Tyler too!" and the election of 1840

Second Great Awakening

Charles G. Finney and the Burned-over District

Joseph Smith, Brigham Young, and Mormonism

Lyman Beecher and the American Temperance Society

Horace Mann

William Lloyd Garrison, *The Liberator,* and the American Anti-Slavery Society

Frederick Douglass

Angelina and Sarah Grimké

John Quincy Adams and the "gag rule"

Elizabeth Cady Stanton, Lucretia Mott, and the Seneca Falls convention

Copyright © Houghton Mifflin Company. All rights reserved.

penitentiaries, the "Auburn system," and the "Pennsylvania system"

Dorothea Dix

Robert Owen and New Harmony

transcendentalists, Brook Farm, and *The Dial*

John Humphrey Noyes and Oneida

Multiple-Choice Questions

Circle the letter of the item that best completes each statement or answers the question.

1. The immediate result of Andrew Jackson's distribution of federal funds to state banks was to
   a. bring about rapid economic expansion, speculation, and inflation.
   b. increase the power of the Second Bank of the United States.
   c. make the purchase of land more difficult.
   d. increase the effectiveness of the Specie Circular.

2. The *South Carolina Exposition and Protest* was drawn up in opposition to the
   a. Missouri Compromise.
   b. spoils system.
   c. Tariff of Abominations.
   d. Compromise of 1833.

3. Which one of the following was founded as a utopian community?
   a. Lexington, Massachusetts
   b. Rochester, New York
   c. Concord, Massachusetts
   d. Oneida, New York

4. Which of the following statements about William Lloyd Garrison is *incorrect*?
   a. He favored the removal of freed blacks from the United States to colonies in Africa.
   b. He opposed abolitionists who wanted to start a political party and run candidates for office.
   c. He favored giving women equal positions and influence with men in the antislavery movement.
   d. He insisted that slavery was sinful and its continued existence unacceptable.

5. The "gag rule" was repealed in 1845 largely due to the efforts of
   a. Theodore Weld.
   b. Horace Mann.
   c. John Quincy Adams.
   d. Andrew Jackson.

6. Which of the following democratic political reforms was adopted between the 1790s and the 1820s?
   a. the removal of gender qualifications for voting
   b. the elimination of property qualifications for voting
   c. the removal of racial qualifications for voting
   d. the lowering of the voting age to eighteen

7. Andrew Jackson's supporters charged that a "corrupt bargain" had been made by
   a. John Quincy Adams and Henry Clay, to make Adams president and Clay secretary of state.
   b. Henry Clay and John C. Calhoun, to undermine Jackson and secure passage of the Compromise of 1833.
   c. Henry Clay and Daniel Webster, to secure recharter of the Second Bank of the United States.
   d. John C. Calhoun and John Quincy Adams, to get Jackson punished for his unauthorized raid on Spanish Florida.

8. Revivalists and Unitarians were similar in
   a. the social classes that they appealed to.
   b. their emotionalism.
   c. their belief that human behavior could be changed for the better.
   d. the cities and towns where most of their followers lived.

9. Reformers of the antebellum period
   a. were usually Democrats rather than Whigs.
   b. were often inspired by the writings of Karl Marx.
   c. rarely advocated legal coercion to force people to live morally.
   d. received their best response in New England and/or areas where New Englanders had migrated.

10. The Seneca Falls Declaration of Sentiments called for
    a. state tax support for public schools.
    b. equal rights for women.
    c. the immediate abolition of slavery.
    d. humane treatment of the mentally ill and establishment of insane asylums for their care.

11. Which of the following was Martin Van Buren *not* associated with?
    a. creating one of the first Democratic state party machines, the Albany Regency
    b. signing the Independent Treasury Bill, which provided for deposit of federal funds in government vaults
    c. serving as president during a severe economic depression
    d. defecting to the newly formed Whig party in protest over Andrew Jackson's handling of the nullification crisis

120   Chapter 10

12. Which of the following quotations is *not* correctly paired with its source?
    a. "Our Union: It must be preserved." John C. Calhoun's *South Carolina Exposition and Protest*
    b. It makes "the rich richer and the potent more powerful." Andrew Jackson's veto message of the recharter of the Bank of the United States
    c. "I will not equivocate—I will not excuse—I will not retreat a single inch—AND I WILL BE HEARD." William Lloyd Garrison's *The Liberator*
    d. "All men and all women are created equal." The Declaration of Sentiments of the Seneca Falls convention

Essay Questions

1. Andrew Jackson deserves to be ranked among the United States' greatest presidents. Accept or refute this statement, and back up your position with a discussion of Jackson's policies and actions as president.

2. Discuss the origins and development of the second American party system. Which parties were involved? Who supported each of them? What did these parties stand for? What impact did their actions have on voter interest and participation in politics?

3. Discuss antebellum reform movements. Who participated? What inspired the reformers? What assumptions did they make? What were their aims and accomplishments?

4. Discuss the rise of "popular religion" in the antebellum United States. In what ways did religious doctrine become democratized? What assumptions did the new theologies make? How did these assumptions affect religious, social, and political life?

5. Compare and contrast the positions of Jacksonian Democrats and Whig supporters of Henry Clay's American System on the issues of the proper role of the federal government, protective tariffs, internal improvements, and banking. How do you account for their similarities and differences?

Answers to Multiple-Choice Questions

1a. Yes. See page 194.
1b. No. Removal of funds from the Second Bank of the United States and placement of those funds in state banks killed the Second Bank.
1c. No. The expansion of credit for a while made the purchase of land much easier.
1d. No. The Specie Circular was issued to try to stop some of the harmful effects of the over-expansion of credit made possible by the deposits in state banks.

2a. No. Had nothing to do with the Missouri Compromise.
2b. No. Nothing to do with it.
2c. Yes. See page 191.
2d. No. That came after Calhoun's protest was published.

3a. No. Town founded in colonial period.
3b. No. A port city and industrial center.
3c. No. See 3a.
3d. Yes. See page 205.

4a. Yes. This statement is incorrect. Garrison opposed removal of freed blacks as opposed to the earlier American Colonization Society. See page 201.
4b. No. This statement is correct. Garrison was opposed to taking abolitionism into party politics.
4c. No. This statement is correct. Garrison was a supporter of equal rights for women.
4d. No. This statement is correct.

5a. No. He was an abolitionist, but he was not a member of Congress.
5b. No. He was an education reformer and not a member of Congress.
5c. Yes. See page 205.
5d. No. Jackson was president, not a member of Congress. Besides, he favored the gag rule.

6a. No. Not done until passage of 19th Amendment in 1919.
6b. Yes. See page 187.
6c. No. Not done until passage of 15th Amendment in 1870.
6d. No. Not done until passage of 26th Amendment in 1971.

7a. Yes. See page 188.
7b. No. Clay and Calhoun did not cooperate on that issue.
7c. No. Both were supporters of the Second Bank of the United States, but they were not accused of a corrupt bargain on that issue.
7d. No. In fact, John Quincy Adams had defended Jackson's actions.

8a. No. Revivals appealed to the poor and uneducated; Unitarianism to the wealthier and more educated.
8b. No. Unitarians did not approve of the emotionalism of Revivalists.
8c. Yes. See page 198.
8d. No. Unitarianism was strongest in New England. Revivalism in places like western New York and on the frontier.

9a. No. Just the opposite.
9b. No. Most often they were inspired by Christian religious idealism.
9c. No. Since they were sure they were doing God's work, they were often quite ready to coerce people to be moral.
9d. Yes. See page 200.

10a. No. Was not about education reform.
10b. Yes. See page 204.
10c. No. Was not about slavery.
10d. No. Was not about mental health reform.

11a. No. He did create one of the first state party machines.
11b. No. As president he did sign the Independent Treasury Bill.
11c. No. He did serve as president during a depression brought on in part by the moves of his predecessor.
11d. Yes. Van Buren stayed a loyal Democrat, who served as Jackson's vice-president during Jackson's second term and then followed him into the White House.

12a. Yes. This quote was taken from Andrew Jackson, not Calhoun, who refused to give unconditional support to the Union. See page 192.
12b. No. Correctly paired.
12c. No. See 12b.
12d. No. See 12b.

Copyright © Houghton Mifflin Company. All rights reserved.

CHAPTER 11
Life, Leisure, and Culture, 1840–1860

Outline

I. **Technology and Economic Growth**
   A. *Introduction*
      1. U.S. pride and belief in progress through improved technology
      2. Technology that transformed life in the antebellum United States: steam engine, cotton gin, mechanical reaper, interchangeable parts, sewing machine, telegraph
      3. Technological advances undermine position of skilled artisans but raise standard of living of many Americans: cotton gin revives slavery
   B. *Agricultural Advancement*
      1. John Deere's steel-tipped plow (1837) simplifies cutting of prairie sod
      2. Cyrus McCormick's mechanical reaper (1834) makes wheat harvesting faster, easier
      3. Use of better animal feed and fertilizers makes farming more efficient in Northeast and South
   C. *Technology and Industrial Progress*
      1. Impact of U.S. system of manufacturing and improved machine tools: mass production, reduced labor cost, lower prices
      2. New inventions put into mass production speedily
      3. Samuel F. B. Morse's telegraph (1844) leads to 15,000 miles of telegraph lines connecting far-flung cities by 1850s
   D. *The Railroad Boom*
      1. Railroads are symbol of democratic progress through technology
      2. Early railroad travel unsafe and uncomfortable
      3. Growth of the rail network (1840–1860) so great that by 1860 United States has more tracks than the rest of the world; railroad technology and service also improve
      4. Impact of railroad expansion on the Midwest: stimulates settlement, agriculture, growth of towns, industrialization of Chicago and Minneapolis
      5. Financing of railroad building makes Wall Street leading capital market in the United States
   E. *Rising Prosperity*

Life, Leisure, and Culture, 1840–1860 123

    1. Technology improves life by lowering prices, increasing purchasing power
    2. Growth of towns and cities provides more work opportunities and income for urban labor

II. The Quality of Life
  A. *Introduction*
    1. Technological advances improve quality of life for middle class; they now enjoy luxuries formerly reserved to the rich
    2. Change slower to reach poor; contrast between life of poor and middle class greater
    3. Medical knowledge lags behind strides made in industry and agriculture; Americans look to popular health fads for prevention and cure of illness

  B. *Dwellings*
    1. Brick row houses become typical urban dwellings; poorest ones are divided up for many families, called tenements
    2. Mass produced furniture allows upper and middle class to fill their homes with rococo furnishings
    3. Increased rental, decreased home ownership in cities
    4. Rural housing on the frontier is one-room log cabin; longer settled areas replace log cabins with wood frame houses

  C. *Conveniences and Inconveniences*
    1. Coal-burning stoves make cooking more convenient, but foul the environment
    2. Majority of homes lack ice boxes and running water, so most Americans eat salted meat and bathe rarely
    3. Cities have poor sewage and sanitation systems; depend on outdoor privies

  D. *Disease and Health*
    1. Yellow fever, cholera, other epidemic diseases spread
    2. Medical professionals and public do not understand causes of epidemic diseases
    3. Crawford Long and William T. Morton pioneer use of ether for anesthesia, but danger of infection in surgery remains great because of poor sanitary practices

  E. *Popular Health Movements*
    1. Hydropathy: the "water cure" becomes popular
    2. Sylvester Graham convinces many road to health is no meat, alcohol, sex; lots of wholegrain bread, vegetables, fruits

  F. *Phrenology*
    1. Analyzing character by feeling bumps and depressions on the skull becomes most popular "scientific" fad
    2. Phrenology appeals to Americans as quick way to assess and improve character

III. Democratic Pastimes
  A. *Newspapers*

Copyright © Houghton Mifflin Company. All rights reserved.

1. U.S. newspapers pre-1830s: little news, small circulation, subsidized by political factions
2. Changes made in newspapers by technology and innovative journalists: lower price, mass circulation, "gripping news stories," big profits
3. James Gordon Bennett fathers the penny press
4. Bennett's *New York Herald* and Horace Greeley's *New York Tribune* also pioneer modern financial and political news reporting

B. *The Theater*
1. Antebellum theater appeals to Americans of all classes
2. Theater audiences rowdy: New York City riot (1849)
3. Melodramas and adaptations of William Shakespeare's plays most popular

C. *Minstrel Shows*
1. Popular in 1840s and 1850s
2. White men performing in blackface
3. Reinforces whites' stereotypes of blacks

D. *P. T. Barnum*
1. Most successful purveyor of popular entertainment
2. Opens American Museum in New York City (1841)
3. Museum intended to entertain, not to educate; panders to public's hunger for new wonders

IV. The Quest for Nationality in Literature and Art

A. *Introduction*
1. Ralph Waldo Emerson leading advocate of an American national literature and art
2. Emerson's "American Scholar" speech (1837) calls for American intellectual independence from Europe; creation of new artistic standards
3. Emerson's transcendentalism an American form of romanticism
4. Transcendentalist ideas: intuition and emotion more important than intellect; all people, not just educated elite, capable of discovering truth and beauty

B. *The American Renaissance*
1. 1820–1860, American Renaissance, "a flowering of art and literature"
2. Most evident in New England and New York
3. In his novels James Fenimore Cooper introduces unique American character, the frontiersman
4. Emerson, in his essays, searches for truth by following his feelings; his disciple Henry David Thoreau preaches right to defy unjust government policies in *Civil Disobedience* (1849) and assails American materialism in *Walden* (1854)
5. Margaret Fuller combines transcendentalism and feminism in *Women in the Nineteenth Century* (1845)
6. Walt Whitman, in *Leaves of Grass* (1855), breaks new ground with lusty, bold poetry in free verse that celebrates American common man

Life, Leisure, and Culture, 1840–1860

C. Hawthorne, Melville, and Poe
1. Do not set works in the United States of their day or focus on common man
2. Share pessimistic view of human nature
3. Develop distinctively American fiction exploring psychological state of characters and essence of human nature
4. Hawthorne: *The Scarlet Letter* (1850), *The House of Seven Gables* (1851)
5. Melville: *Typee* (1846), *Moby-Dick* (1851)
6. Poe: short stories, including "The Fall of the House of Usher" (1839)

D. Literature in the Marketplace
1. Most nineteenth-century United States authors attempt to make a living from their literary work
2. Poe sells short stories to popular magazines
3. Emerson and Melville make money by lecturing for lyceums
4. Some women earn excellent living by writing sentimental novels, such as Susan Warner's *The Wide, Wide World*

E. American Landscape Painting
1. The Hudson River school (1820–1870s): Thomas Cole, Asher Durand, Frederic Church
2. U.S. wilderness depicted with drama and vivid color
3. George Catlin paints Native Americans as "noble savages" before advancing white civilization overtakes them
4. Landscape architects try to bring idealized nature to cities with "rural" cemeteries and parks
5. Grandest imitation countryside park: New York City Central Park, designed by Frederick Law Olmsted and Calvert Vaux

Vocabulary

The following terms are used in Chapter 11. To understand the chapter fully, it is important that you know what each of them means.

despoliation stripping of riches or resources, ruining

machine tools machines that shape metal products

real income (real wages) how much one's income or wages will purchase, given the prices at the time

tenements subdivided houses or apartment houses in the poor, crowded parts of large cities

rococo a style of architecture and decoration originating in France about 1720 and distinguished by abundant and elegant ornamentation

stereotype a characteristic or set of characteristics, usually negative, attributed to all members of a group

archetype original pattern or model; prototype

poll tax a tax that must be paid to exercise the right to vote

Identifications

After reading Chapter 11, you should be able to identify and explain the historical significance of each of the following:

Cyrus W. Field
John Deere's steel-tipped plow and Cyrus McCormick's mechanical reaper
American System of manufacturing, or interchangeable parts
Samuel F. B. Morse
Crawford Long and William T. Morton
hydropathy
Sylvester Graham
phrenology
James Gordon Bennett, the *New York Herald,* and the penny press
Horace Greeley and the *New York Tribune*
P. T. Barnum and the American Museum
minstrel shows
Ralph Waldo Emerson and "The American Scholar"
transcendentalism
James Fenimore Cooper
Edgar Allan Poe
American Renaissance
Henry David Thoreau
Nathaniel Hawthorne
Walt Whitman
Herman Melville
Thomas Cole, Asher Durand, Frederic Church, the Hudson River School, and George Catlin
lyceums
Frederick Law Olmsted, Calvert Vaux, and Central Park

Multiple-Choice Questions

Circle the letter of the item that best completes each statement or answers the question.

1. The 1840s and 1850s in the United States were characterized by all of the following *except*
   a. heightened literary and artistic output and inventiveness.
   b. advances in medical knowledge that lessened the danger and frequency of epidemics.
   c. improvements in transportation and increases in productivity that raised the standard of living for the middle class.
   d. heightened interest in "scientific" and health fads, such as hydropathy and phrenology.

2. Which of the following were inventions of the antebellum period that were mass-produced and/or widely used in the 1840s and 1850s?
   a. the mechanical reaper, the telegraph, the sewing machine
   b. the telephone, the light bulb, the phonograph
   c. the washing machine, the refrigerated railroad car, the steam engine
   d. the radio, the typewriter, the printing press

3. Which of the following statements about the railroads prior to the Civil War is correct?
   a. They hurt agriculture in the Midwest by diverting land away from farming and into railroading and other industries.
   b. They copied business methods used earlier by the builders of turnpikes and canals.
   c. Despite the spectacular expansion of the rail network in the 1850s, as late as 1860 the total value of freight carried by canals was twice as great as that going by rail.
   d. To raise capital, they sold their stock on the New York Stock Exchange, thus helping to make Wall Street the country's leading capital market.

4. Which of the following cities declined in importance as a commercial center because of the railroad building that took place in the 1840s and 1850s?
   a. Atlanta
   b. Chicago
   c. Chattanooga
   d. New Orleans

5. An urban middle-class home by 1860 would probably have
   a. indoor faucets supplying hot and cold running water.
   b. conspicuously ornamented furniture.
   c. an electric refrigerator.
   d. electric lights.

6. James Gordon Bennett was the
   a. founder of the American Museum.
   b. inventor of the cylindrical steam-driven press.
   c. founder of the penny press.
   d. founder of the lyceums.

7. Which of the following statements about transcendentalism is *incorrect*?
   a. It was an American form of romanticism.
   b. It claimed that knowledge of God and truth were born in each individual.
   c. It claimed that great literature must conform to classical standards of form and beauty.
   d. It claimed that a new democratic republic could produce art and literature as great as the old traditional societies of Europe.

8. The part of the nation that produced the greatest number of and most influential writers during the American Renaissance was
   a. the South.
   b. New England and New York.
   c. the mid-Atlantic states.
   d. the Midwest.

9. Which of the following writers introduced into fiction the character of the American frontiersman?
   a. Herman Melville
   b. Edgar Allan Poe
   c. James Fenimore Cooper
   d. Nathaniel Hawthorne

10. Which of the following writers defended the right to disobey unjust laws, criticized the materialism of U.S. society, and doubted the beneficial effects of technological advances?
    a. Walt Whitman
    b. Henry David Thoreau
    c. John Greenleaf Whittier
    d. James Fenimore Cooper

11. The Hudson River school refers to
    a. a famous lyceum established in Albany, New York.
    b. a group of New York writers, including James Fenimore Cooper and Herman Melville.
    c. a group of landscape painters, including Thomas Cole and Frederic Church, who sought to capture on canvas the natural grandeur of the American wilderness.
    d. a group of New York doctors who believed in the miasm theory of the spread of epidemics.

12. In designing New York's Central Park, Frederick Law Olmsted and Calvert Vaux
    a. copied the lay-out of English formal gardens.
    b. tried to create the look of the countryside and screen out the surrounding city.
    c. celebrated the excitement and vitality of urban America by including museums, sports arenas, and other entertainment facilities.
    d. catered to the tastes and interests of the upper class by making the park resemble the grounds of the Palace of Versailles.

Essay Questions

1. In the 1830s Ralph Waldo Emerson called for a probing exploration of American nationality in literature and art. To what extent did the writers and painters of the American Renaissance answer that call?

2. What technological advances were made in agriculture, industry, and transportation between 1830 and 1860? How did these affect the daily lives of antebellum Americans? What impact did these have on the environment?

3. "The bright possibilities rather than the dark potential of technology impressed most antebellum Americans." To what extent did Americans' lives and experiences between 1830 and 1860 justify that attitude?

4. Discuss the rise of popular culture between 1830 and 1860, including the penny press, the sentimental novel, theater and minstrel shows, and popular health and science movements. How did technological advances of the period affect popular culture?

5. How did new technology and an expanded marketplace affect artistic and intellectual life in America between 1840 and 1860? How did artists and intellectuals feel about these changes?

Answers to Multiple-Choice Questions

1a. No. There was heightened literary and artistic output. This was the period of the American Renaissance in literature and art.
1b. Yes. There were few medical breakthroughs during this period. Neither medical professionals nor the public understood the causes of the epidemics that swept through cities periodically. See page 214.
1c. No. Such improvements did take place in the 1840s and 1850s.
1d. No. Americans were very interested in these fads in the period.

2a. Yes. See page 208.
2b. No. All of these were invented in the last quarter of the nineteenth century.
2c. No. The washing machine and refrigerated railroad car were invented post-Civil War and the steam engine predated 1840.
2d. No. The radio and typewriter were invented post-Civil War and the printing press predated 1840.

3a. No. Just the opposite. They stimulated Midwestern agriculture by making it possible for farmers to get their grain and other produce to markets in the East and Europe easily.
3b. No. They could not get state tax money for building as the canals did and they needed much more capital than the earlier ventures.
3c. No. Just the opposite. By 1860 railroads carried much more freight than canals.
3d. Yes. See page 212.

4a. No. Because it was a railroad hub its commercial importance and size grew markedly.
4b. No. See 4a.
4c. No. See 4a.
4d. Yes. See pages 211-212.

5a. No. Almost no homes had that during the period.
5b. Yes. See page 213.

Copyright © Houghton Mifflin Company. All rights reserved.

5c. No. Those were not sold widely until the 1920s.
5d. No. Thomas Edison did not invent the incandescent electric light until 1879.

6a. No. That was P. T. Barnum.
6b. No. He did not invent it, but saw how the new technology could change the newspaper business drastically.
6c. Yes. See page 216.
6d. No. Ralph Waldo Emerson and other New England intellectuals promoted the lyceums as a way to bring new ideas and culture to the public.

7a. No. This statement is correct.
7b. No. See 7a.
7c. Yes. This statement is *incorrect*. The transcendentalists rejected the classical standards. See pages 218-219.
7d. No. See 7a.

8a. No. Probably the South's being overwhelmingly agricultural was not conducive to producing writers.
8b. Yes. See page 219.
8c. No. The fact that the big publishing companies were in Boston and New York tended to attract writers from other areas to New York and Boston.
8d. No. Probably much of the Midwest was still too close to the frontier stage to produce many writers.

9a. No. He wrote more about the human condition in varied settings.
9b. No. His works depended more on exploring psychological states of characters in various settings.
9c. Yes. See page 219.
9d. No. He wrote more about the moral dilemmas and psychological states of characters in varied settings.

10a. No. Whitman celebrated just about everything about American society but slavery.
10b. Yes. See pages 219-220.
10c. No. In his poems he did not deal with these particular issues.
10d. No. Cooper did not advocate civil disobedience and was ambivalent about technological progress.

11a. No. Had nothing to do with lyceums.
11b. No. Did not refer to writers.
11c. Yes. See page 222.
11d. No. Had nothing to do with doctors.

12a. No. They saw such formality as out of place in America.
12b. Yes. See page 222.
12c. No. They believed countrylike parks in cities were necessary to let urban dwellers escape the noise, dirt, and other stressful conditions of the city.
12d. No. See 12a.

CHAPTER 12
The Old South and Slavery, 1800–1860

Outline

I. King Cotton

   A. *Introduction*
   1. 1790s, decline of profitability of tobacco
   2. Cotton culture revives southern agriculture
   3. Reasons for spread of cotton culture: demand from British textile industry, removal of Native Americans from South and Southwest

   B. *The Lure of Cotton*
   1. Grows well in South's climate
   2. Little capital required to become cotton farmer
   3. Cotton growing, when combined with corn and hog production, eliminates need to import food

   C. *Ties between the Lower and Upper South*
   1. Slavery in, and slave trading between, the two regions
   2. Migration from Upper to Lower South
   3. White South's political benefits from Constitution's three-fifths clause
   4. Southern resentment of abolitionist attacks on slavery

   D. *The North and South Diverge*
   1. South: rural, cash-crop agriculture, limited industrialization, capital invested in land and slaves
   2. North: increasingly urban, industrial, capital invested in factories
   3. South slower to develop public schools; has higher rate of illiteracy
   4. Agricultural South: no need for literate work force; fear of educating slaves

   E. *Cotton and Southern Progress*
   1. North views South as backward
   2. Old South not economically backward, just different

II. Social Relations in the White South

   A. *Introduction*

1. Southern society mixes aristocratic and democratic, premodern and modern elements
2. Landownership widespread; big planters socially and politically dominant

B. The Social Groups of the White South
1. 1860, one-fourth of white families slaveowners
2. Four white social groups: planters, small slaveholding farmers, nonslaveholding family farmers (yeomen), pine-barren folk

C. Planters and Plantation Mistresses
1. Often in debt; always looking for better land, higher efficiency, and profits
2. Frequent moves; isolation from other white planters and their wives
3. Heavy responsibilities of plantation mistresses
4. Stress on planters' wives caused by sexual double standard; mulatto children fathered by their husbands

D. The Small Slaveholders
1. Own fewer than twenty slaves; many more of them than big planters
2. In uplands identify with yeomen: in low country, with planters
3. Move often in search of better land and profits

E. The Yeomen
1. Largest group of southern whites; own no slaves
2. Own 50- to 200-acre farms; most often in upland areas
3. Grow some cash crops and food crops for self-sufficiency
4. Work their own land; sometimes use slaves at harvest time

F. The People of the Pine Barrens
1. About 10 percent of southern whites
2. Own no land, no slaves
3. Squat on land; practice subsistence agriculture
4. Self-sufficient and independent

G. Conflict and Consensus in the White South
1. Planters often Whigs; yeomen, Democrats
2. More consensus than conflict among southern whites: social groups cluster in different regions, landownership widespread, whites do not work for other whites
3. Planters dominate state legislatures, but all white men can vote

H. Conflict over Slavery
1. South's nonslaveholding majority supports slavery
2. Reasons: hopes of becoming slaveowners, best means of controlling socially inferior blacks, fears that emancipation will produce race war

I. The Proslavery Argument
1. Slavery a positive good
2. Slavery sanctioned by history and the Bible
3. Southern black slaves better treated than northern "wage slaves"

The Old South and Slavery, 1800–1860 **133**

   4. South suppresses all antislavery statements; seizes abolitionist literature; smashes antislavery presses
   5. 1830s–1860s, southern churches support slavery

III. Honor and Violence in the Old South
   A. *Violence in the White South*
      1. Violence prevalent in white southerners' daily lives
      2. Fighting and murders more frequent than in North
   B. *The Code of Honor and Dueling*
      1. Source of violence: acute sense of white pride, in large part a demonstration that whites have nothing in common with degraded slaves
      2. Southern gentlemen's code of honor: reputation defended through dueling
   C. *The Southern Evangelicals and White Values*
      1. Conflict in values between southern code of honor and southern evangelical preaching
      2. By 1830 southern evangelicals move closer to values of southern gentlemen ; stop trying to appeal to blacks, women, poor; many white upper class men join southern Methodists, Baptists, Presbyterians

IV. Life under Slavery
   A. *Introduction*
      1. Slavery an exploitative institution; exploits blacks' lives and labor to enrich whites
      2. Slave's treatment dependent on his or her master, kind of agriculture, residence in rural or urban area, century he or she lives in
   B. *The Maturing of the Plantation System*
      1. 1700–1830, changes in slavery because of maturing plantation system
      2. Increase in native-born blacks, more even balance of males and females, more slaves working together on plantations
      3. Rapid natural increase of African-Americans
   C. *Work and Discipline of Plantation Slaves*
      1. Males and females work together in fields
      2. Slaves labor most hours under harshest discipline of any antebellum Americans
      3. Slaves subject to brutality
      4. Slave artisans and house servants have higher status than field hands
   D. *The Slave Family*
      1. Receives no legal protection
      2. Broken up by sale
      3. Sexual demands of white men on slave women
      4. Despite hardships, slave family not destroyed; evolves different kinship patterns from whites
   E. *The Longevity, Health, and Diet of Slaves*

Copyright © Houghton Mifflin Company. All rights reserved.

1. U.S. slaves more even sex ratio, better diet than Brazilian; U.S. slaves live longer, reproduce faster
2. U.S. slaves have shorter life expectancy, higher infant mortality than whites
- F. *Slaves off Plantations*
    1. Greater freedom of movement for city slaves
    2. Slave workers in southern factories, mines, lumbering hired from owners; treated as valuable property
- G. *Life on the Margin: Free Blacks in the Old South*
    1. 1860, South has 250,000 free blacks
    2. Free blacks subject to intensifying legal restrictions
    3. Provide main leadership of freedmen after the Civil War
- H. *Slave Resistance*
    1. Slave rebellions and conspiracies: Gabriel Prosser's (Virginia, 1800); Denmark Vesey's (South Carolina, 1822); Nat Turner's (Virginia, 1831); only Turner's results in death of whites
    2. Reasons for small number of slave revolts: blacks outnumbered, isolated, unarmed, fearful for their families, lacking allies
    3. Runaways common, but seldom manage to get to the North
    4. Furtive resistance: theft, sabotage, arson, work stoppage, poisonings

V. **The Emergence of African-American Culture**
- A. *The Language and Religion of Slaves*
    1. Common language of southern slaves: English pidgin
    2. Southern slaves convert from various African religions to common Christianity
    3. Most southern slaves Baptist or Methodist
    4. Christianity unites blacks; does not make all of them rebellious or servile
    5. Christian message about slavery interpreted differently by whites and blacks
- B. *African-American Music and Dance*
    1. Slaves' hopes and sorrows expressed in shouts, music, and dance
    2. African-American work songs and spirituals voice longing for freedom and deliverance

Vocabulary

The following terms are used in Chapter 12. To understand the chapter fully, it is important that you know what each of them means.

yeoman nonslaveholding family farmers, the Old South's most numerous white class

portico a structure consisting of a roof supported by columns, usually attached to a building as a porch

mulatto offspring of one white parent and one black parent

planter a large landholder, especially one who owned twenty or more slaves; planters comprised a small elite class of the Old South

pidgin a simplified language, with no original, native speakers, in which people of different native languages can communicate

Identifications

After reading Chapter 12, you should be able to identify and explain the historical significance of each of the following:

Nat Turner's rebellion

debate in the Virginia legislature over slavery, 1831–1832

three-fifths clause of the Constitution

proslavery argument

southern code of honor

northern "character"

Gabriel Prosser

Denmark Vesey

Frederick Douglass

Harriet Tubman

Josiah Henson

Underground Railroad

Multiple-Choice Questions

Circle the letter of the item that best completes each statement or answers the question.

1. The majority of white men in the antebellum South were
   a. planters.
   b. small slaveholding farmers.
   c. nonslaveholding family farmers.
   d. merchants or shopkeepers.

2. All of the following were true of planters *except*
   a. they searched constantly for more and better land.
   b. they were often in debt.
   c. they usually managed their own estates.
   d. they almost always built mansions for their families on their plantations.

3. The yeomen farmers of the Old South
   a. were congregated in the upland and hilly regions.
   b. did not grow cash crops for market.
   c. did not have the right to vote.
   d. were generally tenants rather than landowners.

4. Compared to the North, the Old South had a higher
   a. literacy rate.
   b. proportion of its people living in cities.
   c. murder rate.
   d. proportion of its white population working for other whites.

5. Which of the following statements about Nat Turner is correct?
   a. He led a slave rebellion in which more than sixty whites were killed.
   b. He was inspired to lead his uprising after reading copies of William Lloyd Garrison's newspaper *The Liberator*.
   c. Almost nothing is known about his motives because he killed himself rather than submit to capture.
   d. He had been treated with extreme brutality by a string of masters before he rebelled.

6. The black family under slavery
   a. received no legal recognition or protection.
   b. disintegrated.
   c. copied the customs and patterns of white families.
   d. was protected against separation of young children and mothers.

7. Why did the Old South not have more slave revolts?
   a. Blacks were outnumbered by whites almost everywhere in the South and lacked allies and guns.
   b. Blacks had no strong desire for freedom, which they did not understand.
   c. Blacks had no inspired leaders.
   d. Blacks were restrained by strong bonds of loyalty to masters who treated them fairly.

8. Most blacks in the antebellum South
   a. rejected Christianity as the religion of their slave masters.
   b. accepted the preaching of white clergy that slavery was divinely sanctioned.
   c. drew from Christianity the view that slavery was an affliction to test their faith and for which masters would be punished.
   d. became obedient and docile because of the Christian promise of reward in heaven for faithful servants.

9. Which of the following was *not* part of the proslavery argument?
   a. Slavery was economically profitable for the slaveowner.
   b. The institution was a positive good because it kept dangerous and inferior blacks under the control of strong and superior whites.
   c. Southern slaves were better cared for than northern factory workers.
   d. The great civilizations of the past, such as ancient Greece and Rome, were dependent on slave labor.

10. The Old South made little progress toward industrialization because
    a. African slaves proved incapable of working in factories.
    b. southern planters did not choose to switch their capital from land and slaves to factory building.
    c. the North forbade the opening of factories in the South.
    d. the South made so little profit from selling cotton that it could not afford to start new enterprises.

11. Which of the following statements about the white folk of the pine barrens is *incorrect*?
    a. They generally squatted on their land rather than owning it.
    b. They usually favored the institution of slavery though they owned no slaves.
    c. They usually worked for the planters as tenant farmers, sharecroppers, or overseers.
    d. They carried on subsistence farming, supplemented by hunting.

12. Which of the following statements about African-Americans in the Old South is *incorrect*?
    a. Their numbers grew from natural increase rather than continued importation from Africa after 1810.
    b. The majority of them in the 1850s worked on small farms with fewer than ten slaves.
    c. By the eve of the Civil War, about 250,000 blacks were classified as free.
    d. As a group, they worked more hours and under harsher conditions than did any other Americans.

Essay Questions

1. Compare and contrast economic, social, and political developments in the North and South between 1800 and 1860. How do you account for the divergence between the two regions?

2. Discuss the white social structure of the Old South. How egalitarian was it? What social groups existed? What was their relationship to each other and to the institution of slavery?

3. The great majority of white southerners never owned a single slave, yet the majority supported the institution of slavery. Write an essay explaining why.

4. Was slavery in the South essentially a paternalistic institution in which most slaves were treated reasonably well, or was it primarily an exploitative institution? Back up your conclusions by citing as much evidence as possible.

5. Discuss the emergence of African-American culture in the Old South. In what ways did it draw on the slaves' African experiences? In what ways did it incorporate the American slave experience? How did it differ from white southern culture and values?

6. Chapter 12 of your textbook states, "Fear of slave insurrection haunted the Old South." Write an essay on slave resistance. How realistic were the fears of whites? What forms did African-American resistance take? Why?

Chapter 12

Answers to Multiple-Choice Questions

1a. No. They were a very small elite group.
1b. No. They were in the minority.
1c. Yes. See page 230.
1d. No. They were a very small group in the mostly agricultural South.

2a. No. This statement is true.
2b. No. See 2a.
2c. No. See 2a.
2d. Yes. This statement is false. See page 229.

3a. Yes. See page 231.
3b. No. They almost always grew some cash crops for market.
3c. No. By the 1830s all white men in the South had the right to vote.
3d. No. They owned their own land.

4a. No. Much lower.
4b. No. See 4a.
4c. Yes. See page 233.
4d. No. See 4a.

5a. Yes. See page 223.
5b. No. There is no evidence that Turner ever saw *The Liberator*.
5c. No. He was captured and stood trial. He gave his court-appointed lawyer his *Confessions*, which say much about his motives.
5d. No. He made no claims that he had been brutalized by his masters.

6a. Yes. See page 236.
6b. No. It became more dependent on extended family and "fictive" kin networks.
6c. No. The nuclear, father-headed family of whites was impossible for slaves to maintain because of sale and other separations.
6d. No. There was no such protection. Young children were frequently separated from their mothers.

7a. Yes. See page 239.
7b. No. All evidence points to blacks having great desire for freedom.
7c. No. There were inspired leaders like Nat Turner and Denmark Vesey.
7d. No. Few slaves felt strong bonds of loyalty to the masters who exploited their labor.

8a. No. Most became Christians, but interpreted the meaning of true Christianity quite differently from their masters.
8b. No. They did not accept that teaching of white clergy.
8c. Yes. See pages 240-241.
8d. No. Nat Turner and other leaders of conspiracies and rebellions often claimed to be inspired by their reading and understanding of the Bible.

9a. Yes. Though slavery was economically profitable for the slaveowners, they seldom admitted that was the justification for the "peculiar institution."
9b. No. This was a part of the proslavery argument, especially used to impress nonslaveholders.
9c. No. This was a part of the proslavery argument.
9d. No. See 9c.

10a. No. Most of the labor in factories that did exist in the South, such as the Tredegar Iron Works, was supplied by slaves.
10b. Yes. See page 227.
10c. No. The North did not.
10d. No. Quite the opposite. They made so much money from selling cotton that they had no incentive to invest in factories.

11a. No. This statement is correct.
11b. No. See 11a.
11c. Yes. This statement is *incorrect*. White folk of the pine barrens did not work for other whites. See page 231.
11d. No. See 11a.

12a. No. This statement is correct.
12b. Yes. This statement is *incorrect*. The majority worked on plantations with more than 20 slaves. See page 235.
12c. No. See 12a.
12d. No. See 12a.

CHAPTER 13
Immigration, Expansion, and Sectional Conflict, 1840–1848

Outline

I. **Newcomers and Natives**

　A. *Introduction*
　　1. 1840–1860, 4.2 million immigrants enter the country
　　2. Majority of immigrants from Ireland and Germany

　B. *Expectations and Realities*
　　1. Immigrants seeking economic betterment
　　2. Majority of immigrants in 1840–1860, settle in cities
　　3. Irish in Northeast work in construction, railroad building; Germans in Midwest, varied occupations

　C. *The Germans*
　　1. German immigrants represent diverse religions, classes, occupations
　　2. German language binds them
　　3. Cluster in German neighborhoods; build ethnic institutions
　　4. Native-born Americans admire Germans' industriousness, criticize their clannishness

　D. *The Irish*
　　1. Three waves of Irish immigration: 1815–1820s, many Protestants and middle class; 1820s–1840s, more Catholics and poorer; 1845–1850s, mostly Catholics fleeing potato blight and famine
　　2. Enter work force at the bottom
　　3. Compete with blacks; animosity between the two groups

　E. *Anti-Catholicism, Nativism, and Labor Protest*
　　1. Heavy Catholic immigration produces Protestant backlash; 1840s, nativist, anti-Catholic, anti-immigrant societies form
　　2. 1850s, a nativist society, Order of the Star-Spangled Banner, becomes Know-Nothing party, an important political force
　　3. 1844, anti-Catholic "Bible Riots" in Philadelphia

Immigration, Expansion, and Sectional Conflict, 1840–1848 **141**

   4. Nativists consider Catholicism undemocratic; native-born workers fear job competition from Catholic immigrant workers
   5. Native-born artisans and middle class demand land reform
   6. Limited success of early labor unions; legal sanction gained from *Commonwealth* v. *Hunt* (1842)
 F. *Labor Protest and Immigrant Politics*
   1. Democratic party preference of German and Irish immigrants
   2. Reasons for preference: Democrats seen as for common people; Whigs seen as aristocratic, abolitionist, anti-Catholic, and protemperance
   3. Democratic party appeals to immigrants to support U.S. territorial expansion as in their best interest

II. The West and Beyond
 A. *The Far West*
   1. 1820s–1840s, Southwest belongs to Mexico; Great Britain and United States occupy Oregon jointly
   2. 1820s, U.S. line of settlement no farther than Missouri
 B. *Far Western Trade*
   1. 1790s–1820s, U.S. merchants establish trading posts on West Coast
   2. St. Louis merchants trade with Southwest
 C. *Spanish and American Settlement in the West*
   1. Spanish mission system declines after 1830
   2. Conflicts between Mexicans and Native Americans discourage Mexican settlement
   3. 1820s, Mexico encourages U.S. citizens to settle in Texas; by 1830 twice as many Americans as Mexicans in Texas
   4. 1830s, Mexican attempts to halt further U.S. entry and stop slavery fail
   5. Texan-Americans resent Mexican restrictions
 D. *The Texas Revolution*
   1. 1835, Antonio López de Santa Anna's army occupies Texas
   2. 1835, Americans in Texas rebel
   3. 1836, Defeat of Americans at Alamo; 1836, Sam Houston's victory at San Jacinto
   4. Texas declares independence; Mexico refuses to recognize
 E. *American Settlements in California, New Mexico, and Oregon*
   1. 1840s, Americans stream into Sacramento Valley
   2. 1840, more than 500 U.S. settlers in Oregon
 F. *The Overland Trail*
   1. Dangers arising from unknown, difficult terrain; poor guidebooks; the Donner party
   2. Pioneers on the trail travel together in wagon trains, share work and protection
   3. 1840–1848, 11,500 Americans settle in Oregon; 2,700 in California

III. The Politics of Expansion

A. *The Whig Ascendancy*
   1. William Henry Harrison and the Whigs win election of 1840
   2. Harrison dies; Vice President John Tyler, states' rights former Democrat, takes over
   3. Tyler vetoes all Whig economic legislation

B. *Tyler and Texas Annexation*
   1. Tyler attempts to gain popularity with success in foreign policy
   2. Tyler and Secretary of State John C. Calhoun sign treaty annexing Texas; 1844, Calhoun writes letter defending slavery
   3. Senate rejects treaty; northerners fear annexation a plot to spread slavery

C. *The Election of 1844*
   1. Whig nominee Henry Clay waffles on Texas annexation
   2. Democratic nominee James K. Polk calls for "reannexation of Texas"
   3. Reasons for Polk's victory: defection of some northern Whigs to Liberty party, Catholic and immigrant votes for the Democrats

D. *Manifest Destiny*
   1. Election of 1844 demonstrates growing support for expansion
   2. John L. O'Sullivan, journalist, coins term Manifest Destiny (1845)
   3. Believers in Manifest Destiny argue United States must spread free institutions from coast to coast, acquire markets for its produce, increase trade with Asia, gain new land for farmers, avoid class strife within heavy urban populations
   4. The penny press and immigrants favor expansionism

E. *Polk and Oregon*
   1. In 1844 campaign, Polk calls for U.S. annexation of Oregon
   2. Polk and Senate accept compromise treaty of 1846 dividing Oregon with British at forty-ninth parallel

F. *The Origins of the Mexican War*
   1. 1845, Congress annexes Texas
   2. Polk claims Rio Grande, not Nueces River, is Texas boundary
   3. Polk sends John Slidell to Mexico to negotiate to buy California and New Mexico
   4. Mexico refuses to sell; Polk orders U.S. troops into disputed region south of the Nueces
   5. Zachary Taylor's forces and Mexican troops clash; Polk asks Congress to declare war on Mexico
   6. Minority in United States accuses Polk of proslavery aggression; majority backs war

G. *The Mexican War*
   1. 1847, Taylor beats Mexicans at Buena Vista
   2. 1846, Stephen Kearney conquers New Mexico
   3. U.S. conquest of California: John C. Frémont and the Bear Flag Republic; Commodore John D. Sloat's naval victories; Kearney's invasion from New Mexico
   4. 1847, Winfield Scott takes Mexico City

5. Treaty of Guadalupe-Hidalgo (1848): Mexico recognizes Rio Grande boundary and cedes to the United States Texas, New Mexico, and California as well as parts of Nevada, Utah, Arizona, Colorado, Wyoming; United States pays citizens' claims against Mexico and pays Mexico $15 million

H. *Intensifying Sectional Divisions*
   1. 1846–1848, sectional conflict sharpens
   2. Conflict erupts over Polk's economic policies and spread of slavery into New Mexico and California
   3. Whigs oppose spread of slavery on moral grounds, and northern Democrats want to keep land for free white settlers

I. *The Wilmot Proviso*
   1. Introduced by David Wilmot, northern Democrat
   2. Calls for prohibiting slavery in territory taken from Mexico, other than Texas
   3. Calhoun and southerners claim Constitution protects right of owners to take slave property into all territories
   4. Northerners back proviso; point to precedent of Northwest Ordinance

J. *The Election of 1848*
   1. Whigs nominate Zachary Taylor; no platform
   2. Democrats nominate Lewis Cass; back "squatter sovereignty" or "popular sovereignty"
   3. Free-Soilers (pro-Wilmot Proviso Democrats, Liberty party abolitionists, "Conscience Whigs") nominate Martin Van Buren; no expansion of slavery
   4. Taylor wins; big Free-Soil vote shows popularity in North of stopping slavery's spread

K. *The California Gold Rush*
   1. Gold discovered in California
   2. By December 1848 gold rush begins
   3. Flood of prospectors in California makes question of slavery in the West of "immediate practical concern"

Vocabulary

The following terms are used in Chapter 13. To understand the chapter fully, it is important that you know what each of them means.

freethinker one who has rejected authority and ritual, especially in religion, in favor of rational inquiry and speculation

nativism dislike and suspicion of immigrants; the policy of protecting the interests of native inhabitants versus those of immigrants

secularization transferring control or ownership of something from the church or religious authorities to civil authorities, such as the government

tenuous flimsy, weak

dark horse a little-known or unlikely political figure who unexpectedly wins nomination and/or election

proviso a clause in a statute, contract, or the like by which a condition is introduced; a stipulation or condition

Identifications

After reading Chapter 13, you should be able to identify and explain the historical significance of each of the following:

Know-Nothing party

Commonwealth v. *Hunt* (1842)

Tammany Hall

Philadelphia "Bible Riots"

Spanish missions and presidios

Stephen F. Austin and American *empresarios* in Texas

Antonio López de Santa Anna

the Alamo

Sam Houston

Overland Trail and the Donner party

Californios

John Tyler

John C. Calhoun

Henry Clay

James K. Polk

John L. Sullivan and Manifest Destiny

Zachary Taylor

Winfield Scott

John C. Frémont and the Bear Flag Republic

Treaty of Guadalupe-Hidalgo

Wilmot Proviso

Lewis Cass and squatter or popular sovereignty

Martin Van Buren and the Free-Soil Party

Skill Building: Maps

On the map of the western United States, locate each of the following and explain its historical significance:

forty-ninth parallel

Great Plains

Rocky Mountains

Oregon Territory

54°40´ latitude

St. Louis

Santa Fe

Santa Fe Trail

Texas and the Mexican cession

Sacramento valley

Columbia River

Vancouver Island

Rio Grande

Nueces River

San Francisco

36°30´ latitude

Multiple-Choice Questions

Circle the letter of the item that best completes the statement or answers the question.

1. The two biggest sources of immigration to the United States between 1840 and 1860 were
   a. Italy and eastern Europe.
   b. China and Japan.
   c. Ireland and the German states.
   d. Great Britain and Scotland.

2. In the case of *Commonwealth* v. *Hunt* (1842), the Massachusetts Supreme Court ruled that
   a. slavery was unconstitutional in Massachusetts.
   b. labor unions were not necessarily illegal combinations or monopolies.
   c. Massachusetts tax money could not be used to support an unjust war against Mexico.
   d. segregated schools for blacks in Massachusetts did not violate the U.S. Constitution.

3. Squatter or popular sovereignty meant
   a. allowing residents of a territory to decide whether to permit slavery there.
   b. extending the right to vote to all male settlers in the Far West.
   c. deciding the ownership of a territory by vote of its residents.
   d. the right of Native Americans to keep the lands they were already cultivating.

4. Which of the following statements about President James K. Polk's actions is *incorrect*?
   a. He sent John Slidell to Mexico with an offer to buy California and New Mexico.
   b. He ordered Zachary Taylor to keep his troops north of the Nueces River to avoid a confrontation with Mexico.
   c. He agreed to split the Oregon Territory with the British at the forty-ninth parallel, although he had demanded all of it during his presidential campaign.
   d. He signed a bill lowering the tariff and vetoed one giving federal aid for internal improvements.

5. The expansionist phrase *manifest destiny* was coined by
   a. John Tyler
   b. Sam Houston.
   c. John C. Frémont.
   d. John L. O'Sullivan.

6. The fate of the Donner party best illustrates
   a. the hazards faced by pioneers traveling west on the Overland Trail.
   b. the lack of appeal of abolitionism to the majority of immigrants.
   c. the widespread lack of interest among Americans in Henry Clay's American System by the 1840s.
   d. the vicious attacks on Catholics and immigrants that took place in the 1830s and 1840s.

7. Irish and German immigrants in the 1840s were most likely to
   a. vote for Whig candidates for office because of their identification with temperance and other reform movements.
   b. be nativists and join the Know-Nothings.
   c. join the abolitionist movement and vote for the Liberty party.
   d. vote for Democrats, whom they perceived as sympathetic to the common people and antiprivilege.

8. The Senate rejected the treaty annexing Texas that was drawn up by Secretary of State John C. Calhoun because
   a. he defended annexation as a way to protect and defend slavery.
   b. the Texans made it clear that they were not yet ready to give up their independence and join the United States.
   c. Great Britain threatened to break off diplomatic relations if the United States took the territory without compensating them.
   d. Mexico threatened to declare war on the United States if it stole Mexico's province.

9. The Wilmot Proviso called for
   a. annexing Texas.
   b. prohibiting slavery in territory acquired from Mexico.
   c. extending the Missouri Compromise line of 36°30′ to the West Coast.
   d. passing legislation to limit immigration into the United States.

10. Presidios were
    a. agents who contracted with the Mexican government to bring U.S. settlers into Texas.
    b. Mexicans who owned huge ranches worked by enslaved Native Americans.
    c. Franciscan priests who endeavored to convert Native Americans to Christianity.
    d. forts constructed by the Spanish to protect their missions in the Southwest.

11. The Free-Soil party in the election of 1848
    a. nominated the war hero Zachary Taylor and swept to victory.
    b. did well enough in the North to show that the majority of northerners had become abolitionists by then.
    c. gained enough votes for its candidate, Martin Van Buren, to demonstrate the widespread opposition in the North to the spread of slavery into the territories.
    d. won enough votes for its nominee, Lewis Cass, to demonstrate the widespread popularity of squatter sovereignty with poor working people.

12. In which of the following sets are the historical events arranged in correct chronological order?
    a. Texas declares independence; United States annexes Texas; United States declares war on Mexico; Treaty of Guadalupe Hidalgo is signed
    b. Gold is discovered in California; United States offers to buy California from Mexico; Mexico declares war on the United States; United States annexes Texas and California
    c. U.S. settlers in California revolt against Mexico; United States declares war on Mexico; Texans are killed at the Alamo; Treaty of Guadalupe-Hidalgo is signed
    d. Texans defeated at the Alamo; United States offers to buy Texas from Mexico; Mexico declares war on the United States; United States forces clash with Mexican troops in the area between the Rio Grande and Nueces River

Essay Questions

1. Discuss immigration to the United States in the 1840s and 1850s. Who came? Why did immigrants come? Where did they settle? What economic and political roles did they play?

2. Discuss the rise of anti-Catholic and nativist sentiment and movements in the United States in the 1840s. What caused them? Who supported such groups? What impact did these groups have on U.S. politics?

3. What did expansionists mean by the term *manifest destiny*? What arguments did they use to justify expansion? To whom did these arguments appeal? Why?

4. Discuss the causes of the Mexican War. To what extent did the United States provoke the confrontation? Why did some members of Congress and the public oppose the war?

5. Explain the following statement with as much illustrative evidence as possible: "[E]xpansion brought sectional antagonism to the boiling point, split the Democratic party in the late 1840s, and set the nation on the path to the Civil War."

Answers to Multiple-Choice Questions

1a. No. Not until after 1880.
1b. No. Very limited Chinese and Japanese immigration during the 1840s.
1c. Yes. See page 244.
1d. No. Some, but not nearly as heavy as Irish and German.

2a. No. Decision had nothing to do with slavery.
2b. Yes. See page 248.
2c. No. No court ever took that position.
2d. No. Did not deal with that issue.

3a. Yes. See pages 261-262.
3b. No. Did not deal with which men could or could not vote.
3c. No. Ownership of the Mexican Cession had been decided by conquest in war.
3d. No. It offered nothing to Native Americans.

4a. No. The statement is correct.
4b. Yes. Polk purposely ordered Taylor to move his troops into the disputed territory in hopes of provoking war with Mexico as a way of gaining New Mexico and California. See page 257.
4c. No. See 4a.
4d. No. See 4a.

5a. No. He hoped to gain popularity by pushing expansion, but he didn't make up the phrase.
5b. No. He led the Texan revolt against Mexico, but he didn't make up the phrase.
5c. No. He led the uprising of Americans in California, but he didn't make up the phrase.
5d. Yes. See page 255.

6a. Yes. See pages 243-244.
6b. No. Had nothing to do with slavery.
6c. No. Had nothing to do with the American System.
6d. No. Had nothing to do with attacks on immigrants.

7a. No. Both Irish and German immigrants opposed temperance reform.
7b. No. Nativists and Know-Nothings hated immigrants, so they weren't likely to win support of immigrants.
7c. No. The Irish opposed freeing slaves who they feared would then compete with them for jobs.
7d. Yes. See page 248.

8a. Yes. See page 254.
8b. No. Texas was willing to be annexed.
8c. No. Britain took no stand since Texas had never been their territory.
8d. No. Mexico did threaten, but that is not what the Senate was worried about.

9a. No. That had already been done.
9b. Yes. See page 261.
9c. No. That is not what it proposed.
9d. No. Proviso said nothing about immigration.

10a. No. Those were *empresarios*.
10b. No. Not what they were called.
10c. No. They ran the Indian missions and were called *padres*.
10d. Yes. See page 250.

Copyright © Houghton Mifflin Company. All rights reserved.

Chapter 13

11a. No. That was the Whig party.
11b. No. The people who voted for Free-Soil were generally not abolitionists.
11c. Yes. See page 262.
11d. No. Poor working people generally preferred keeping slavery out of western territories and reserving the land for the use of poor white men like themselves.

12a. Yes. Texas declares independence (1836); United States annexes Texas (1845); United States declares war on Mexico (1846); Treaty of Guadalupe-Hidalgo signed (1848).
12b. No. Events are not in the order in which they occurred.
12c. No. See 12b.
12d. No. See 12b.

CHAPTER 14
From Compromise to Secession, 1850–1861

Outline

I. **The Compromise of 1850**
   A. *Introduction*
      1. 1848, United States has equal number of free and slave states
      2. All possible solutions to slavery in Mexican cession controversial
      3. Other issues divide North and South; slavery in Washington, D.C., poor enforcement of Fugitive Slave Act
   B. *Zachary Taylor at the Helm*
      1. President Taylor favors admitting California and perhaps New Mexico as free states
      2. 1850, Southerners protest possibility of two new free states by calling Nashville Convention
   C. *Henry Clay Proposes a Compromise*
      1. Henry Clay proposes compromise bill:
         a. Admit California as free state
         b. Divide rest of Mexican cession into New Mexico and Utah territories; future of slavery up to residents of area (popular sovereignty)
         c. Federal government pays off Texas public debt
         d. Settle Texas–New Mexico border dispute in New Mexico's favor
         e. Continue to allow slavery but not slave trading in Washington, D.C.
         f. Pass and enforce tough new fugitive slave law
      2. Taylor dies; successor Millard Fillmore supports the compromise
      3. Fall 1850, compromise bills pass
   D. *Assessing the Compromise*
      1. Compromise does not settle differences between North and South
      2. North's gains: admission of California as free state; end of slave trading but not slavery in Washington, D.C.
      3. South's gains: tough new fugitive slave law, but it proves less beneficial to slaveowners than hoped
   E. *Enforcement of the Fugitive Slave Act*

1. Law stacks the deck against blacks: denies jury trial, right to testify; pays commissioner more for returning a black to slavery than declaring that person free
2. Northerners oppose enforcement of the law: mobs interfere with fugitives' arrests (1854, Boston, Anthony Burns), citizens form vigilance committees, states pass personal liberty laws

F. *Uncle Tom's Cabin*
1. 1852, Harriet Beecher Stowe publishes *Uncle Tom's Cabin*
2. Sells over one million copies and is turned into play seen by even more people
3. Helps build antislavery feeling in North

G. *The Election of 1852*
1. Whigs nominate Winfield Scott for president; Democrats, Franklin Pierce
2. Democrats rally behind Compromise of 1850 and popular sovereignty
3. Pierce wins by big margin

II. The Collapse of the Second Party System

A. *Introduction*
1. Second party system collapses during Pierce's administration
2. Senator Stephen A. Douglas's popular sovereignty bill for the Nebraska Territory hastens death of the Whigs
3. Strictly sectional Republican party emerges

B. *The Kansas-Nebraska Act*
1. Douglas's Kansas-Nebraska Act (1854) shatters weakened second party system and revives sectional strife
2. Kansas-Nebraska Act repeals Missouri Compromise; divides region into Kansas and Nebraska territories; slavery question to be settled by popular sovereignty
3. Chance that slavery can spread north of 36°30′ line pleases South, infuriates North

C. *The Surge of Free Soil*
1. Free-soilers denounce Kansas-Nebraska Act as plot to spread slavery into all territories
2. Free-soilers not necessarily concerned about blacks
3. Free-soilers want territories as place of opportunity for whites to become self-employed farmers and businessmen

D. *The Ebbing of Manifest Destiny*
1. Kansas-Nebraska Act's possible opening of territories to slavery dampens enthusiasm for expansion in North
2. Pierce has to repudiate Ostend Manifesto and other southern attempts to annex Caribbean and Central American territories

E. *The Whigs Disintegrate*
1. Kansas-Nebraska Act undermines Whig party; Northern Whigs split between antislavery "conscience" Whigs and conservative supporters of Compromise of 1850

2. 1854–1856, many antislavery Whigs and antislavery Democrats first join American (or Know-Nothing) party; then by 1856, switch to Republican party

F. *The Rise and Fall of the Know-Nothings*
   1. Know-Nothing party evolved from nativist Order of the Star-Spangled Banner
   2. Party, combining fear of Catholic conspiracy and Slave Power conspiracy, gains big following, 1854–1855
   3. Northern and southern Know-Nothings split over accepting Kansas-Nebraska Act; antislavery former Whigs and antislavery former Democrats drift out of Know-Nothings and into Republican party

G. *The Origins of the Republican Party*
   1. By 1856 Republicans are main opposition to Democratic party
   2. Republicans united in opposition to Kansas-Nebraska Act; party brings together conservatives who want to keep Missouri Compromise, Liberty party members, abolitionists, and free-soilers
   3. Bleeding Kansas heightens northern free-soil sentiments and augments Republican ranks

H. *Bleeding Kansas*
   1. Proslavery and antislavery whites settle in Kansas
   2. March 1855, neighboring Missouri residents vote illegally in Kansas territorial election; help elect proslavery Lecompton government
   3. Kansas free-staters organize rival antislavery Topeka government
   4. Sack of Lawrence and John Brown's Pottawatomie massacre touch off civil war in Kansas
   5. Pierce administration supports proslavery Lecompton government
   6. Republican senator Charles Sumner denounces proslavery forces; Democratic congressman Preston Brooks assaults Sumner in Senate
   7. Republicans condemn arrogant, aggressive southern aristocrats

I. *The Election of 1856*
   1. Republicans nominate John C. Frémont for president; Southern Know-Nothings, Millard Fillmore; Democrats, James Buchanan
   2. Buchanan wins
   3. Election shows that Know-Nothing party is dead; that Republicans, though lacking followers in the South, can almost win presidency; that Democrats can keep winning if they can hold their northern and southern wings together

III. The Crisis of the Union
   A. *The Dred Scott Case*
      1. March 1857, Supreme Court hands down *Dred Scott* decision
      2. Decision says blacks are not U.S. citizens; Missouri Compromise unconstitutional because Congress cannot exclude slavery from territories; Fifth Amendment protects rights of property holders to take slave property to territories

3. Republicans decry decision and slaveocracy
B. *The Lecompton Constitution*
   1. Buchanan backs proslavery Lecompton constitution in Kansas, asks Congress to admit the state under it
   2. Stephen A. Douglas and other northern Democrats break with Buchanan
   3. Congress refuses to admit Kansas as a slave state
   4. Buchanan fails to pacify Kansas; alienates northern Democrats
C. *The Lincoln-Douglas Debates*
   1. 1858, Republican Abraham Lincoln runs against Douglas for U.S. Senate seat from Illinois
   2. August–October 1858, candidates hold seven debates
   3. Douglas favors popular sovereignty in territories; proclaims "Freeport Doctrine" (settlers can bar slavery from a territory by refusing to enact laws protecting slaveholders)
   4. Lincoln says Congress lacks constitutional power to end slavery in South; he is not in favor of racial equality
   5. Lincoln for barring slavery from all territories; attacks slavery as moral evil
   6. Douglas wins Senate race; election further splits Democratic party; makes Lincoln "famous in the North and infamous in the South"
D. *The Legacy of Harpers Ferry*
   1. South sees John Brown's raid on Harpers Ferry as work of Republican party with backing of most northerners
   2. Raid ignites southern hysteria over slave insurrections; plays into hands of southern extremists
E. *The South Contemplates Secession*
   1. Southerners regard Republican party as menace to southern rights
   2. Southerners resent Republican condemnation of slavery and of southern way of life
   3. As long as doughface Buchanan president, southerners only talk about secession
F. *The Election of 1860*
   1. In response to Panic of 1857 and depression, Republicans develop economic program: protective tariff, federally-funded internal improvements, Homestead Act
   2. Republicans nominate moderate Lincoln for president, thinking he can carry key states of Illinois and Pennsylvania
   3. Democratic party splits; northern Democrats nominate Douglas; southern Democrats, John C. Breckenridge
   4. Some former northern and southern Whigs found Constitutional Union party; nominate John Bell
   5. Lincoln's platform: Congress cannot end slavery in South but must prohibit its expansion into territories
   6. Douglas's platform: slavery in territories should be decided by popular sovereignty
   7. Breckenridge's platform: Congress must allow and protect slavery in all territories

From Compromise to Secession, 1850–1861

  8. Bell's platform: no stand on expansion of slavery
  9. Lincoln wins with majority in electoral college; 39 percent of popular vote, almost all from North
G. *The Movement for Secession*
  1. Many southerners see Lincoln as a dangerous John Brown–type abolitionist
  2. December 20, 1860, South Carolina convention votes for secession; Alabama, Mississippi, Florida, Georgia, Louisiana, Texas secede
  3. February 4, 1861, seven seceded states establish Confederate States of America; choose Jefferson Davis as president
  4. Upper South does not join them
H. *The Search for Compromise*
  1. Senator John J. Crittenden offers compromise to get seceded states back: compensate owners of runaway slaves, repeal personal liberty laws, pass constitutional amendment guaranteeing federal government will never end slavery in South, extend Missouri Compromise line across territories, keep south of the line open to slavery
  2. Lincoln rejects Crittenden compromise: will not abandon Republican free-soil promise, underestimates strength of southern secessionists, will not allow minority to undermine majority rule
I. *The Coming of the War*
  1. March 1861, Lincoln takes office; pledges to hold federal fort, Fort Sumter, in Charleston, South Carolina
  2. April 12, 1861, Confederates attack Fort Sumter
  3. Lincoln proclaims Deep South in rebellion; calls for 75,000 militia to suppress
  4. Virginia, North Carolina, Arkansas, Tennessee secede and join Confederacy
  5. Union and Confederacy close ranks and prepare to battle

Vocabulary

The following terms are used in Chapter 14. To understand the chapter fully, it is important that you know what each of them means.

omnibus bill a bill including numerous items or subjects

conspiracy a secret agreement to perform an evil or unlawful act; a secret plot

capital crime or offense a criminal wrongdoing punishable by death

referendum the procedure of submitting legislative measures directly to the voters for approval or rejection

insurrection an armed uprising or other open resistance against a government or other established authority; a revolt

doughface in the 1850s, a northern politician whose views were acceptable or even sympathetic to the South

vigilantes members of extralegal citizen groups organized to maintain order and punish offenses

Chapter 14

secede to withdraw from a body, such as a nation

Identifications

After reading Chapter 14, you should be able to identify and explain the historical significance of each of the following:

John Brown's raid on Harpers Ferry

doctrines of free soil and free labor

William H. Seward and irrepressible conflict

popular sovereignty

Daniel Webster

Henry Clay's omnibus bill and the Compromise of 1850

Millard Fillmore

Fugitive Slave Act of 1850 and personal liberty laws

Harriet Beecher Stowe, *Uncle Tom's Cabin*

American (or Know-Nothing) party

Stephen A. Douglas and the Kansas-Nebraska Act

Gadsden Purchase

Ostend Manifesto

"Bleeding Kansas"

Lecompton legislature, Topeka legislature, and the Lecompton constitution

sack of Lawrence and Pottawatomie massacre

Charles Sumner and Preston Brooks

John C. Frémont

James Buchanan

Roger B. Taney and *Dred Scott* v. *Sandford*

Lincoln-Douglas debates and Douglas's Freeport Doctrine

Panic of 1857

John C. Breckenridge

John Bell and the Constitutional Union party

Jefferson Davis and the Confederate States of America

Crittenden compromise

Fort Sumter

Skill Building: Maps

On the map of the United States c. 1860, locate and draw in each of the following. How is each related to sectional conflict and the coming of the Civil War?

Missouri

Kansas and Nebraska territories

36°30′ latitude

New Mexico Territory

Utah Territory

California

Gadsden Purchase

states that seceded by February 1861 (Lower South)

states that seceded after fighting at Fort Sumter (Upper South)

border states that did not secede

Charleston, South Carolina

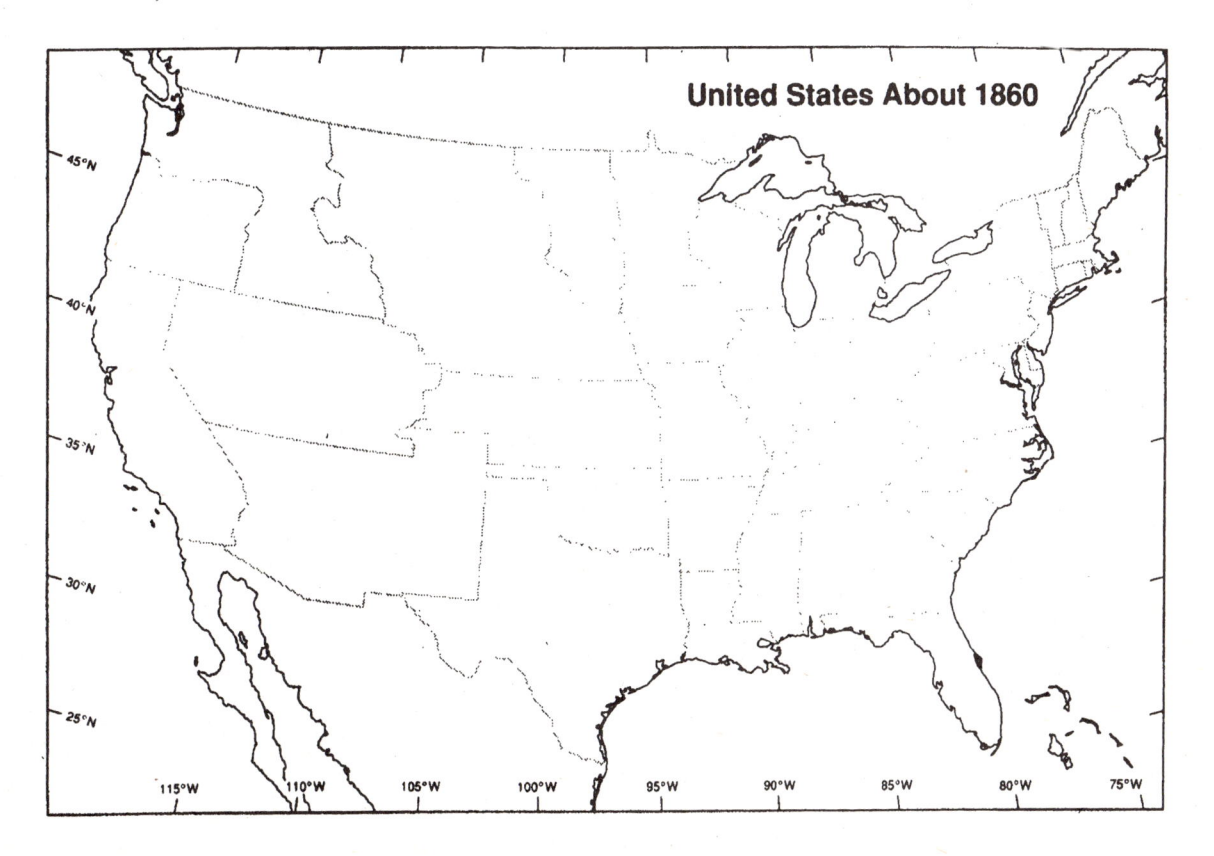

United States About 1860

Multiple-Choice Questions

Circle the letter of the item that best completes each statement or answers the question.

1. Which of the following statements about the Compromise of 1850 is correct?
   a. It ended slavery in Washington, D.C.
   b. It allowed the people of California to decide by popular sovereignty whether to allow slavery.
   c. It had the backing of John C. Calhoun and almost all southerners but was opposed by Daniel Webster and most northerners.
   d. Its passage was helped by the support of Millard Fillmore, who became president after Zachary Taylor's death.

2. Personal liberty laws were
   a. state laws aimed at hampering enforcement of the Fugitive Slave Act.
   b. federal laws guaranteeing slaveholders' right to protection of their slave property.
   c. state laws prohibiting blacks, free or slave, from entering a state.
   d. federal laws guaranteeing that states would not deny any person life, liberty, or property without due process of law.

3. Stephen Douglas's Freeport Doctrine
   a. angered northern Democrats by repudiating popular sovereignty.
   b. angered southern Democrats by pointing out how settlers could effectively exclude slavery from a territory despite the *Dred Scott* decision.
   c. undermined Lincoln's free-soil position by showing that it was unworkable.
   d. helped to unify the Democratic party for the election of 1860.

4. Which is the most valid statement describing the Republican party's position in the election of 1860?
   a. There should be immediate, complete emancipation of slaves in the South.
   b. A program of gradual, compensated emancipation should be started.
   c. There should be no further extension of slavery into the territories.
   d. The principle of popular sovereignty should be applied honestly in the remaining territories.

5. What did the South gain from the Compromise of 1850?
   a. a stronger fugitive slave law
   b. a slave code for the territories
   c. the right to bring slaves into all territories taken from Mexico
   d. a lower tariff

6. The Lecompton constitution would have provided
   a. a policy for the Supreme Court to follow in cases involving slavery.
   b. an independent country in Africa for freed slaves.
   c. a permanent compromise on slavery for future states.
   d. a proslavery government for Kansas.

7. The Ostend Manifesto pertained to
    a. Cuba.
    b. California.
    c. Mexico.
    d. Florida.

8. The *Dred Scott* decision declared that Congress could not
    a. admit new slave states.
    b. prohibit slaveholders from taking slaves into northern states.
    c. bar slavery in the territories.
    d. pass a fugitive slave law.

9. The secession of southern states began immediately after
    a. announcement of the *Dred Scott* decision.
    b. civil war in Kansas.
    c. Lincoln's inauguration.
    d. Lincoln's election.

10. Which of the following statements about the Crittenden compromise is correct?
    a. Although it did not solve the basic differences between North and South, it did postpone the Civil War for ten years.
    b. Lincoln rejected it because he would not abandon the promise of free soil on which he had been elected.
    c. Lincoln was willing to accept it, but the Confederate states felt that it did not open enough new territory to slavery.
    d. Lincoln rejected it because he had decided by 1861 that he was going to issue an emancipation proclamation freeing all slaves.

11. Which of the following was denounced by northerners as "an atrocious plot" to undo the Missouri Compromise and turn the territories into "a dreary region of despotism, inhabited by masters and slaves"?
    a. the Crittenden compromise
    b. the Compromise of 1850
    c. the Kansas-Nebraska Act
    d. the fugitive slave law

12. Which person is *not* correctly matched with his or her work?
    a. John C. Calhoun—the Kansas-Nebraska Act
    b. Henry Clay—the Compromise of 1850
    c. Harriet Beecher Stowe—*Uncle Tom's Cabin*
    d. Roger B. Taney, *Dred Scott* v. *Sandford*

Essay Questions

1. Imagine that you are a Virginia cotton planter or planter's wife in May 1861. Compose a letter to a friend in New York explaining why your state has just seceded from the Union.

2. Repeated sectional compromises in 1820, 1833, and 1850 held the Union together and averted civil war. Why did compromise fail in 1860–1861?

3. Although the Compromise of 1850 postponed secession and civil war for a decade, it also contributed to embittered feelings between the North and the South. Discuss and illustrate this statement.

4. Discuss the birth of the Republican party. How and why did it come about? Who supported it and why? What did it stand for? How and why did it broaden its appeal in the late 1850s?

5. Discuss the demise of the second party system. How is its breakdown related to immigration, nativism, slavery, and the spread of slavery to the West?

Answers to Multiple-Choice Questions

1a. No. It kept slavery, but ended slave trading in Washington, D.C.
1b. No. It allowed California to enter the Union as a free state.
1c. No. Calhoun denounced it and Webster pleaded for it as the only way to avoid civil war.
1d. Yes. See page 268.

2a. Yes. See page 269.
2b. No. They were state, not federal laws, and their intent was to undo the Fugitive Slave Act, not help enforce it.
2c. No. Some northern states had such laws, but they were not called personal liberty laws.
2d. No. These were state, not federal, laws.

3a. No. The doctrine was an attempt to show how popular sovereignty could still work, despite the *Dred Scott* decision. Therefore, it pleased northern Democrats.
3b. Yes. See page 279.
3c. No. Lincoln's free-soil position did not accept popular sovereignty and/or the *Dred Scott* decision.
3d. No. Just the opposite. It drove northern and southern Democrats further apart.

4a. No. The Republican party and Lincoln never took that position until passage of the Thirteenth Amendment.
4b. No. In 1860 Lincoln and the Republican party took the position that the Federal government had no power to touch slavery in the states where it already existed.
4c. Yes. See page 281.
4d. No. That was the position of Stephen Douglas and the northern Democrats.

5a. Yes. See pages 267-268.
5b. No. Not a part of the Compromise of 1850. The South would demand it only after the *Dred Scott* decision and Douglas's Freeport Doctrine.
5c. No. California would enter as a free state, and in the remaining territory taken from Mexico popular sovereignty would decide.
5d. No. That was included in the Compromise of 1833, not 1850.

6a. No. Did not involve the Supreme Court.

6b. No. Had nothing to do with that.
6c. No. It was specific to Kansas, and it certainly didn't compromise on slavery.
6d. Yes. See page 278.

7a. Yes. See page 272.
7b. No. Had nothing to do with California, which had already entered the Union as a free state.
7c. No. Few Americans desired to take over any more of Mexico than they had already grabbed in the Mexican Cession.
7d. No. Had been bought by the United States back in 1819.

8a. No. Not what it said.
8b. No. Both northerners and southerners agreed that the Federal government could not interfere with slavery in states. Therefore, northern states could certainly bar slaves from being brought in to them, and many did.
8c. Yes. See page 276.
8d. No. Not what it said.

9a. No. The southern states were very pleased by the *Dred Scott* decision, which opened all territories to slavery, so they had no motive to leave at that point.
9b. No. They were not ready to leave that soon.
9c. No. The deep South did not wait for Lincoln to be inaugurated. The month after he was elected in November 1860 South Carolina started the wave of deep South states that seceded.
9d. Yes. See page 281.

10a. No. The Crittenden compromise was never agreed to. The statement would be correct if made about the Compromise of 1850.
10b. Yes. See page 282.
10c. No. Lincoln was not ready to accept it because it would destroy the platform on which he had been elected and undermine the principle that policy was determined by the wishes of the majority as expressed in a free and fair election.
10d. No. Lincoln had decided no such thing. He pledged to uphold slavery in the southern states where it already existed.

11a. No. That was proposed later and was never accepted.
11b. No. Northerners were not happy about the Fugitive Slave Act part of the compromise, but the compromise did not directly overturn the Missouri Compromise.
11c. Yes. See page 272.
11d. No. See 11b.

12a. Yes. John C. Calhoun is *not* correctly matched with the Kansas-Nebraska Act. That law was sponsored by Stephen Douglas. See pages 271-272.
12b. No. Clay was the author of the Compromise of 1850, so he is correctly matched.
12c. No. Stowe was the author of *Uncle Tom's Cabin*, so she is correctly matched.
12d. No. Taney did write the *Dred Scott* decision, so he is correctly matched.

CHAPTER 15
Reforging the Union: Civil War, 1861–1865

Outline

I. **Mobilizing for War**

   A. *Recruitment and Conscription*
   1. Union and Confederacy depend on army volunteers at first; policy proves inadequate
   2. April 1862, Confederacy passes conscription law: all able-bodied white men age eighteen to thirty-five subject to draft; owners and overseers of twenty or more slaves exempt
   3. Exemption resented in South; complaints of "a rich man's war but a poor man's fight"
   4. Confederate army has adequate arms but shortages of food, clothing
   5. 1863, South passes Impressment Act: allows Confederate agents to take food and slaves for army use
   6. March 1863, Union passes Enrollment Act: exempts from draft those who pay substitute or pay $300 commutation fee
   7. Exemptions lead to resentment and bounty jumping

   B. *Financing the War*
   1. Both sides sell war bonds and print unbacked paper money
   2. Union greenbacks depreciate less than Confederate dollars because North makes greenbacks legal tender and prints fewer of them than does South
   3. February 1863, Congress also passes National Bank Act: banks can obtain federal charters and issue bank notes

   C. *Political Leadership in Wartime*
   1. Political divisions in the Union: northern Democrats oppose conscription, National Bank, abolition of slavery, centralization of federal power
   2. President Abraham Lincoln caught between northern Democrats and Radical Republicans, who demand immediate emancipation of slaves and stringent reconstruction of South
   3. Political divisions in the Confederacy: Vice President Alexander Stephens and states' righters criticize President Jefferson Davis's centralization of power in effort to win the war

Reforging the Union: Civil War, 1861–1865

    4. Lincoln's superior leadership holds his party and the Union together
    5. Davis's abrasive style and lack of opposition party in Confederacy result in bitter factionalism

  D. *Securing the Union's Borders*
    1. Lincoln safeguards Washington, D.C., by securing border slave states
    2. Lincoln sends federal troops to Maryland and suspends writ of habeas corpus
    3. 1862, Union troops drive Confederate army out of Kentucky
    4. Union and Confederate sympathizers clash in Missouri
    5. Four border slave states (Maryland, Delaware, Kentucky, Missouri) stay in Union

II. In Battle, 1861–1862

  A. *Armies, Weapons, and Strategies*
    1. Union advantages: larger population; more white men of fighting age; control of more than 90 percent of country's industry, two-thirds of railroad track
    2. Confederate advantages: fighting defensive war; battling on home territory means shorter supply lines and higher morale; slave labor force can carry on nonmilitary work; South can use larger percentage of white men for fighting
    3. New weapons in Civil War: submarines, repeating rifles, the Gatling gun
    4. Rise of trench warfare; decline in importance of cavalry
    5. North's Anaconda plan involves blockading southern coast, capturing Mississippi River; Union lacks ships and men to accomplish plan in 1861
    6. West of Appalachians, Union soldiers move south from Kentucky into Tennessee; east of mountains, North attempts to capture Richmond

  B. *Stalemate in the East*
    1. July 1861, Confederates rout Union in First Battle of Bull Run (First Manassas)
    2. Lincoln appoints George B. McClellan commander of the Army of the Potomac
    3. McClellan's Peninsula Campaign to take Richmond from rear foiled by Robert E. Lee's Army of Northern Virginia (Seven Days Battles, June–July 1862)
    4. August 1862, Confederates Lee and Stonewall Jackson win Second Battle of Bull Run (Second Manassas)
    5. September 17, 1862, McClellan turns back Lee's thrust into Maryland at Antietam (Sharpsburg); Lincoln issues Emancipation Proclamation
    6. Lincoln replaces too cautious McClellan with Ambrose Burnside
    7. Burnside fails to take Richmond; loses many soldiers at Fredericksburg
    8. War in eastern theater—a stalemate

  C. *The War in the West*
    1. April 1862, Union troops under Ulysses S. Grant defeat Confederates at Shiloh, Tennessee
    2. April 1862, land-sea force, under Benjamin Butler and Admiral David Farragut, captures New Orleans
    3. Union naval forces take Memphis, Tennessee; by 1863 Union controls Mississippi River except 200 miles between Port Hudson, Louisiana, and Vicksburg, Mississippi

Copyright © Houghton Mifflin Company. All rights reserved.

4. 1862, in the far west, Union forces drive Confederates out of New Mexico and take control of the Missouri River
5. After defeat of Confederates in far west, Union volunteers battle Native Americans in Minnesota, Arizona, Nevada, Colorado, New Mexico

D. *Ironclads and Cruisers: The Naval War*
1. Union builds world's largest navy; tightens naval blockade of South
2. March 1862, battle of the ironclads: *Monitor* versus *Merrimac*
3. Despite damage to northern merchant ships by southern raiders such as *Alabama* and *Florida*, South loses naval war to North

E. *The Diplomatic War*
1. Confederacy hopes to win diplomatic recognition from European countries; thinks British and French will break North's blockade to get cotton
2. 1861, North captures Confederate diplomats James Mason and John Slidell aboard the *Trent*
3. Great Britain threatens war; Lincoln releases Mason and Slidell
4. Union protests British building of commerce raiders (*Alabama* and *Florida*) and ironsides for Confederacy
5. Great Britain and France do not recognize Confederacy: Lincoln's Emancipation Proclamation wins support of British and French public opinion; Great Britain has enough cotton without South's

III. Emancipation Transforms the War

A. *From Confiscation to Emancipation*
1. Lincoln cautious at first about declaring war on slavery; does not want to anger border slave states and northern Democrats
2. August 1861, First Confiscation Act: slaves used in military aid of rebellion will be seized
3. Radical Republicans press Lincoln to free all slaves; point out Confederacy benefiting from slave labor
4. July 1862, Second Confiscation Act: frees slaves of rebels and slaves who cross Union lines; authorizes use of blacks as soldiers in Union army
5. Lincoln stalls on enforcement of Second Confiscation Act, instead issues Preliminary Emancipation Proclamation (September 1862): all slaves in rebel hands to be free as of January 1, 1863
6. Emancipation Proclamation (January 1, 1863) has no immediate impact; frees only slaves in areas not controlled by Union, leaves slavery in border states
7. Emancipation Proclamation satisfies Radical Republicans, wins support for Union in Europe, transforms Civil War into fight against slavery

B. *Crossing Union Lines*
1. 1865, 500,000 former slaves in Union hands
2. Many freedmen serve as Union army cooks, laborers, spies, scouts

Copyright © Houghton Mifflin Company. All rights reserved.

3. Many white Union soldiers very prejudiced, but as blacks help army, whites become more accepting
4. March 1865, Freedmen's Bureau established to educate, aid former slaves
5. Bureau authorized to lease forty acres of land confiscated from rebels to each freedman or loyal white

C. *Black Soldiers in the Union Army*
1. Large-scale enlistment of black soldiers after Emancipation Proclamation
2. One-tenth (186,000) of all Union soldiers African-Americans
3. Discrimination against black troops: serve in segregated units commanded by whites, have higher mortality rate than whites, not treated as prisoners of war when captured by Confederacy, paid less than whites until 1864
4. Blacks serve bravely; see military service as validation of their U.S. citizenship

D. *Slavery in Wartime*
1. Southerners try to control slaves by increased patrols, moving them away from Union lines, telling them Yankees will hurt them
2. Majority of blacks, when they get the chance, flee to Union lines
3. Slaves on plantations refuse to work; destroy property; slave system breaks down

E. *The Turning Point of 1863*
1. Summer–fall 1863, Union gains important victories
2. July 1863, Lee's invasion of Pennsylvania stopped at Gettysburg
3. July 1863, Grant captures Vicksburg; Port Hudson, last Confederate stronghold on Mississippi, falls
4. November 1863, Union takes Chattanooga, ready to march into Georgia
5. Union victories shore up North's will to fight, bring despair to some Confederates

IV. War and Society, North and South

A. *The War's Economic Impact: The North*
1. War-related industries and railroads boom in North
2. Republican-dominated Congress passes probusiness measures: higher protective tariffs (1862, 1864), Pacific Railroad Act (charter, subsidies, land to Union Pacific and Central Pacific), national banking system
3. Free-soil, free-labor legislation: Homestead Act (1862) and Morrill Land Grant Act (1862)
4. Contractors make fortunes speculating and selling "shoddy" goods
5. Workers suffer, wages lag behind inflation; increased use of low-paid child and female laborers

B. *The War's Economic Impact: The South*
1. War undermines South's economy: railroads destroyed, cotton and food production decline
2. Confederacy seizes food from civilians to feed army; Confederate soldiers desert to protect their starving families

Chapter 15

   3. Southern planters grow cotton, rather than food, to trade to northern buyers
C. Dealing with Dissent
   1. Internal dissent in Union and Confederacy
   2. Confederacy: Appalachian nonslaveholding farmers and states' rights politicians denounce Jefferson Davis's government
   3. Union: peace Democrats (Copperheads) criticize Emancipation Proclamation and growth of federal power, demand immediate peace with South
   4. Peace Democrats strongest in border states, Midwest, and among immigrant urban workers
   5. 1863, New York City draft riot: Irish workers attack blacks, draft offices, rich Republicans
   6. Lincoln tougher on dissenters than Davis; Lincoln suspends writ of habeas corpus and imposes martial law several times
   7. 1866, Supreme Court rebukes Lincoln in *Ex parte* Milligan: rules that civilians cannot be tried by military tribunals when regular civil courts are open
D. The Medical War
   1. U.S. Sanitary Commission, run by women volunteers, raises money for medical supplies and extra food for Union army
   2. 3,200 women serve as nurses to Union and Confederate troops; for Union, Dorothea Dix, Clara Barton; for Confederates, Belle Boyd
   3. Limited medical knowledge leads to frightful death toll from disease and infected wounds
   4. Grim conditions in prisoner-of-war camps; Andersonville, Georgia, worst
E. The War and Women's Rights
   1. 1863, Elizabeth Cady Stanton and Susan B. Anthony organize National Woman's Loyal League
   2. Feminists demand end of slavery, the vote for blacks and women
   3. Civil War does not change women's inferior political, economic, social status

V. The Union Victorious, 1864–1865
   A. The Eastern Theater in 1864
      1. Lincoln puts Ulysses S. Grant in command of all Union armies, 1864
      2. Grant moves his headquarters to eastern theater; attacks Lee in Virginia; orders William T. Sherman to invade Georgia
      3. May, June, heavy casualties at Battle of Wilderness and Cold Harbor; Grant pushes on, forces Lee to pull back to trenches outside Petersburg and Richmond
      4. Grant dispatches General Philip Sheridan to Shenandoah Valley; Sheridan devastates and controls it by September
   B. Sherman in Georgia
      1. Sherman invades Georgia while Grant battles Lee in the Wilderness
      2. September 2, 1864, Sherman takes Atlanta

Reforging the Union: Civil War, 1861–1865

- C. The Election of 1864
    1. To win votes of prowar Democrats, Republicans change name to National Union party; nominate Lincoln for president, southern Unionist Democrat Andrew Johnson for vice president
    2. Democrats nominate George B. McClellan; platform calls for immediate peace with South
    3. September, fall of Atlanta helps reelect Lincoln in November
- D. Sherman's March through Georgia
    1. Sherman burns Atlanta, marches across Georgia to Savannah
    2. Sherman's army lives off countryside and seizes or destroys everything of value in its path
    3. December 1864, Sherman takes Savannah; continues into North Carolina
- E. Toward Appomattox
    1. By spring 1865 Confederate morale broken, men deserting in droves
    2. April 3, 1865, Union forces enter Richmond
    3. Remains of Lee's army flee westward to Lynchburg
    4. Grant and Sheridan cut off escape route; Lee surrenders to Grant at Appomattox Courthouse
    5. April 14, John Wilkes Booth shoots Lincoln; April 15, Lincoln dies

Vocabulary

The following terms are used in Chapter 15. To understand the chapter fully, it is important that you know what each of them means.

conscription compulsory enrollment of men for military or naval service; the draft

gross national product (GNP) the sum, measured in dollars, of all goods and services produced in a given year

writ of habeas corpus a formal order requiring that an arrested person be brought before a judge or court and either charged with a specific crime or released; the right to such a writ is guaranteed in the U.S. Constitution

reconnaissance a search in the field to uncover useful military information

bigotry intolerant attachment to a particular belief, prejudice, or opinion

dissent to disagree with the opinions and policies of the government, church, or social majority

martial law law imposed on an area by military forces when civil authority has broken down or been pushed aside

feminist an advocate of equality for women in political, economic, and social life

Identifications

After reading Chapter 15, you should be able to identify and explain the historical significance of each of the following:

20–Negro law

bounty jumpers

Legal Tender Act and greenbacks

National Bank Act (1863) and national bank notes

Jefferson Davis

Charles Sumner, Thaddeus Stevens, and the Radical Republicans

the Anaconda plan

first and second battles of Bull Run (First and Second Manassas)

George B. McClellan

Thomas "Stonewall" Jackson

Robert E. Lee

Battle of Antietam (Sharpsburg)

Ulysses S. Grant

ironclads and the battle of the *Merrimac* and the *Monitor*

Trent affair

First and Second Confiscation Acts and Emancipation Proclamation

Fort Pillow massacre

Gettysburg, Pennsylvania

Vicksburg, Mississippi

Pacific Railroad Act, 1862

Homestead Act, 1862

Morrill Land Grant Act, 1862

Copperheads and Clement L. Vallandigham

New York City draft riot, 1863

Ex parte Milligan, 1866

Elizabeth Cady Stanton, Susan B. Anthony, and the National Woman's Loyal League

William T. Sherman

National Union party and Andrew Johnson

Appomattox Courthouse, Virginia

Copyright © Houghton Mifflin Company. All rights reserved.

Skill Building: Maps

On the map of the southeastern United States, locate each of the areas or places listed below. What is the political and/or military importance of each in the Civil War?

western theater
eastern theater
Appalachian Mountains
Mississippi River
Richmond, Virginia
Washington, D.C.
Shenandoah Valley
Maryland
Missouri
Kentucky
Memphis, Tennessee
Vicksburg, Mississippi
Gettysburg, Pennsylvania
Atlanta, Georgia
route of Sherman's march to the sea

Multiple-Choice Questions

Circle the letter of the item that best completes each statement or answers the question.

1. Lincoln's Emancipation Proclamation
   a. freed the slaves in the slave states that remained in the Union.
   b. freed the slaves in the western territories.
   c. freed the slaves in areas in rebellion against the U.S. government.
   d. freed all slaves in the Union and Confederacy.

2. Which of the following Union military objectives proved the hardest and took the longest to accomplish?
   a. taking Richmond
   b. gaining control of the Mississippi
   c. taking New Orleans
   d. taking Atlanta

3. Andrew Johnson was nominated as Lincoln's running mate in 1864 to
   a. please the Radical Republicans.
   b. win the votes of prowar northern Democrats.
   c. influence the South to rejoin the Union because he would be a southern vice president.
   d. reward Tennessee for remaining loyal to the Union.

4. Which of the following men denounced Lincoln's Emancipation Proclamation and suspension of the writ of habeas corpus and called for immediate peace with the Confederacy?
   a. Thaddeus Stevens
   b. Salmon Chase
   c. Clement L. Vallandigham
   d. Charles Sumner

5. The Union capture of Vicksburg and Port Hudson was strategically important because
   a. it opened the way to Richmond.
   b. it completed Union control over the Atlantic coast.
   c. it gave Lincoln the victories he was waiting for to issue the Emancipation Proclamation.
   d. it gave the North control over the whole Mississippi River.

6. The Supreme Court ruled in *Ex parte* Milligan that
   a. civilians could not be tried by military tribunals when the civil courts were open.
   b. Lincoln had no constitutional right to free slaves in the Confederacy.
   c. the Union had no right to confiscate rebel leaders' property.
   d. Congress rather than the president had the right to direct the reconstruction of the South.

7. Slaves during the Civil War
   a. overwhelmingly remained loyal to their masters and to the South.
   b. often served as officers in the Union army over other blacks.
   c. ran to Union lines when they could and worked for or fought for the North.
   d. were never allowed to enlist as soldiers in either the Union or the Confederate armies.

8. Which of the following statements is correct?
   a. Jefferson Davis's government did *not* try to gain recognition from European countries because it did *not* want to encourage European intervention in U.S. affairs.
   b. Great Britain and France built ships for the Confederacy, recognized it, and sent small numbers of troops to the United States to help the Confederacy defend itself against Union attacks.
   c. Great Britain did *not* recognize the Confederacy because the British had less need for southern cotton than the South anticipated, and Lincoln's Emancipation Proclamation won sympathy for the Union from the British working and middle classes.
   d. Great Britain needed southern cotton so badly that it repeatedly attacked the northern blockade of the South and nearly went to war against the Union.

9. Which of the following statements about women in the Civil War is correct?
   a. Women were *not* allowed to enter army camps to nurse soldiers.
   b. Women replaced draftees in many of the industrial jobs in the North.
   c. Loyal Unionist women were allowed to vote and run for political office.
   d. Northern missionary and freedmen's aid societies refused to use women volunteers.

10. Which of the following statements is correct?
    a. Both the Union and the Confederacy printed unbacked paper money to help finance their war efforts.
    b. The Union had to resort to conscription to get enough soldiers, but the Confederacy recruited enough volunteers to avoid imposing the draft.
    c. Neither the Union nor the Confederacy exempted the wealthy from the draft.
    d. Both the Union and the Confederacy ruthlessly suppressed all internal dissent for the duration of the war.

11. In 1863, Irish workers in New York City rioted because
    a. the Republican-dominated Congress passed laws cutting off further Irish immigration into the United States.
    b. Lincoln refused to allow Irish and other immigrants to join the Union army, while enlisting native-born African-Americans.
    c. they resented being drafted while the rich could buy their way out of serving, and the Irish did not want to fight to free blacks.
    d. native-born white Protestant soldiers were better paid than immigrant Catholic troops.

12. By 1865, African-Americans constituted about what portion of the Union army?
    a. One-tenth
    b. One-fourth
    c. Three-fourths
    d. One-twentieth

Essay Questions

1. In his 1861 inaugural address, Lincoln said, "I have no purpose, directly or indirectly, to interfere with the institution of slavery in the states where it exists." In September 1862 he issued his preliminary Emancipation Proclamation. Explain why and how this marked change of policy took place.

2. Discuss the military advantages and disadvantages of each side at the start of the Civil War. Considering that the preponderance of advantages belonged to the Union, why did the North take four years to defeat the South?

3. Compare and contrast the economic impact of the Civil War on the Union and the Confederacy.

4. The Civil War has been called a second American Revolution, an event that significantly transformed the nation's social, economic, and political fabric. Write an essay agreeing or disagreeing with that assessment, and offer as much evidence as possible to back up your position.

5. Pretend that you are one of the following: a northern young man or woman working in a factory, the wife of a Confederate soldier, or a rank-and-file Confederate soldier. Write a journal entry or letter, based on the content of Chapter 15, explaining your attitudes, experiences, hardships, aspirations, and complaints.

Answers to Multiple-Choice Questions

1a. No. It left slavery untouched in those states.
1b. No. That had already been done.
1c. Yes. See page 297.
1d. No. That was accomplished by the Thirteenth Amendment.

2a. Yes. Not accomplished until April 1865. See page 307.
2b. No. Done by summer 1863.
2c. No. Done in 1862.
2d. No. Done by September 1864.

3a. No. They did not like the idea of a former Democrat and southerner on the Republican ticket.
3b. Yes. See page 306.
3c. No. There was no hope of that.
3d. No. Tennessee was one of the states that seceded and joined the Confederacy.

4a. No. He was one of the leading Radical Republicans.
4b. No. See 4a.
4c. Yes. See page 303.
4d. No. See 4a.

5a. No. Not related by geography or any other way.
5b. No. Vicksburg and Port Hudson are on the Mississippi River, not the Atlantic coast.
5c. No. Lincoln issued the preliminary Proclamation after the battle of Antietam.

5d. Yes. See page 300.

6a. Yes. See page 303.
6b. No. Not what the case was about.
6c. No. See 6b.
6d. No. See 6b.

7a. No. The evidence proves the opposite.
7b. No. Blacks in the Union army always served under white officers.
7c. Yes. See pages 297 to 299.
7d. No. The Emancipation Proclamation gave blacks the right to join the Union army and by the end of the war, one-tenth of the Union soldiers were African-American.

8a. No. The Confederacy tried very hard to gain recognition from European countries.
8b. No. Britain and France never recognized the Confederacy and gave it no help other than building some ships for it.
8c. Yes. See page 296.
8d. No. The British did not need southern cotton that badly because they found alternative suppliers in India and Egypt.

9a. No. They often did just that.
9b. Yes. See pages 302 and 304.
9c. No. Women won no new political rights as a result of the Civil War.
9d. No. They relied heavily on women volunteers.

10a. Yes. See pages 288-289.
10b. No. Both North and South imposed the draft.
10c. No. They both did.
10d. No. Neither did.

11a. No. Congress did no such thing.
11b. No. The Irish and other immigrants were encouraged to join, and many did.
11c. Yes. See page 303.
11d. No. But until 1864 white troops were better paid than black.

12a. Yes. See page 297.
12b. No. Too high.
12c. No. See 12b.
12d. No. Too low.

CHAPTER 16
The Crises of Reconstruction, 1865–1877

Outline

I. **Reconstruction Politics**

   A. *Lincoln's Plan*

      1. December 1863, Lincoln issues Proclamation of Amnesty and Reconstruction: southern states can form new governments after 10 percent of white voters take loyalty oath to Union and recognize end of slavery; no provision for black suffrage
      2. July 1864, Congress passes Wade-Davis bill: to form new government, 50 percent of voters take loyalty oath and recognize end of slavery; all who cooperated with Confederacy excluded from new governments
      3. Lincoln pocket-vetoes bill; at time of his death, he and Congress at impasse on southern reconstruction

   B. *Presidential Reconstruction under Johnson*

      1. May 1865, President Andrew Johnson announces his plan of southern reconstruction
      2. Provisions of Johnson plan: whites take loyalty oath, establish new governments; new governments proclaim secession illegal, repudiate Confederate debt, ratify Thirteenth Amendment (abolishing slavery); former Confederate officeholders, military leaders, and well-to-do barred from participating until pardoned by president
      3. Summer 1865, Johnson hands out pardons wholesale
      4. Former Confederate leaders and large planters dominate new governments created under Johnson's plan
      5. Some new governments refuse to ratify Thirteenth Amendment and show intention to make black freedom nominal by passing "black codes"
      6. Many northerners horrified at southern defiance
      7. December 1865, Republican-dominated Congress refuses to recognize new southern governments or seat the men they send to House and Senate

   C. *Congress versus Johnson*

      1. Congress tries to get rid of black codes and protect blacks' basic civil rights by extending life of Freedmen's Bureau and passing Civil Rights Act of 1866
      2. Johnson's vetoes of these measures drive moderate Republicans into cooperation with Radical Republicans

3. Together, moderates and radicals plan constitutional amendment to protect provisions of Civil Rights Act
D. *The Fourteenth Amendment*
   1. April 1866, Congress passes Fourteenth Amendment
   2. Provisions: All persons born or naturalized in United States are citizens; state cannot abridge rights of citizens without due process of law or deny equal protection of the law; states that deny black men the vote can have their representation in Congress reduced; former Confederate officials excluded from voting and officeholding; Confederate debt repudiated, federal debt upheld
   3. Fourteenth Amendment first federal attempt to make states respect citizens' civil and political rights
   4. Johnson denounces amendment, campaigns against it
   5. 1866, Republican defenders of amendment win big majorities in congressional elections; have mandate for amendment and their Reconstruction program
E. *Congressional Reconstruction*
   1. Congress passes Reconstruction Act of 1867 over Johnson's veto
   2. Provisions: Invalidates state governments formed under Lincoln and Johnson plans; divides ten former Confederate states (Tennessee already readmitted to Union) into five military districts; states write new constitutions under military supervision; new constitutions must give black men the vote; after Congress approves a state's constitution and the state ratifies Fourteenth Amendment, state is readmitted to Union
   3. Congress does not approve Radical Republican plan to redistribute land
   4. Johnson tries to thwart congressional Reconstruction by appointing conservative military officers; Republicans decide Johnson must be stopped from interfering
F. *The Impeachment Crisis*
   1. March 1867, Congress passes Tenure of Office Act to keep Johnson from removing Radical Republican secretary of war Edwin Stanton
   2. August 1867, Johnson suspends Stanton; February 1868, Johnson tries to fire Stanton
   3. House votes charges of impeachment; March 1868, Senate begins trial
   4. Some Republicans hesitate, fearing removal of president for political reasons will destroy constitutional balance of power
   5. Seven Republicans vote not guilty; Senate vote is one short of necessary two-thirds for conviction
G. *The Fifteenth Amendment*
   1. Fifteenth Amendment, passed 1869, aims to protect southern blacks, extend suffrage to northern blacks, gain new voters for Republican party
   2. Amendment provides that right to vote cannot be denied because of race, color, or previous condition of servitude
   3. Women's rights leaders Elizabeth Cady Stanton and Susan B. Anthony denounce Congress for not extending vote to women as well as black men

4. By 1870 Fifteenth Amendment ratified, along with Thirteenth and Fourteenth; all former Confederate states readmitted to Union

II. Reconstruction Governments

A. *A New Electorate*
   1. Reconstruction laws (1867–1868) create new electorate in South by enfranchising over 700,000 blacks; 15 percent of whites disenfranchised
   2. New electorate puts into power Republican governments made up of carpetbaggers (northerners who resettle in South), scalawags (white small farmers, often former Unionists), blacks
   3. Carpetbaggers and scalawags hold most political offices

B. *Republican Rule*
   1. Achievements/policies of Republican Reconstruction governments:
      a. democratize southern politics: provide universal manhood suffrage
      b. reject land distribution
      c. establish public school systems (segregated), increase public services, undertake extensive public works
   2. New services and rebuilding cost more money, lead to higher taxes; southern landowners object to increased taxes, accuse governments of waste, corruption
   3. On the whole, southern state governments less corrupt than northern ones of the period

C. *Counterattacks*
   1. White southern Democrats organize to drive Republican Reconstruction governments from power
   2. Democrats appeal to scalawags; organize terrorist groups such as Ku Klux Klan
   3. Terrorist groups begin campaign of violence and intimidation against black voters, Freedmen's Bureau officials, white Republicans
   4. 1870–1871, Congress passes Enforcement Acts to suppress violence; not enough federal troops in South to enforce laws, stop violence; 1869, Freedmen's Bureau ends
   5. Vigilantism succeeds in suppressing black vote, toppling most Republican Reconstruction governments

III. The Impact of Emancipation

A. *Confronting Freedom*
   1. Former slaves leave plantations; search for family members separated by past sales
   2. Reunited husbands and wives marry legally; great majority of African-Americans establish two-parent families

B. *African-American Institutions*
   1. Blacks establish churches that play major religious, social, and political roles; black ministers become most important community leaders
   2. With aid from Freedmen's Bureau and northern philanthropists, African-Americans establish schools and universities: Howard, Atlanta, Fisk, Hampton Institute
   3. Segregation of all facilities in South becomes way of life

4. 1883, Supreme Court, in Civil Rights Cases, declares unconstitutional the Civil Rights Act of 1875, banning segregation
   C. Land, Labor, and Sharecropping
      1. Freedmen want to become independent landowners
      2. Few of them succeed because federal government rejects land reform and blacks have no capital; southern whites want to keep blacks as cheap source of agricultural labor
      3. Landless laborers and landholding planters develop form of tenantry known as sharecropping
      4. 1880, 80 percent of land in cotton states farmed by sharecroppers
   D. Toward a Crop-Lien Economy
      1. Local merchants sell supplies to sharecroppers and tenants on credit, with lien on sharecroppers' or tenants' share of crop as collateral
      2. Sharecroppers must pay landlord large part of crop as rent; rest of and sometimes more than its value, owed to credit merchant because of exorbitant interest rates and padded accounts
      3. Southern farmers, as a result, fall into perpetual debt; are forced to live on credit and continue to produce easily sold, soil-depleting cash crop (cotton)
      4. Sharecropping and crop-lien systems impoverish southern agriculture

IV. **New Concerns in the North**
   A. Grantism
      1. Election of 1868: Republicans nominate Ulysses S. Grant; Democrats, Horatio Seymour; Grant wins with help of black vote in South
      2. Grant administration and many state and local governments marred by corruption; Jay Gould, Jim Fisk, and Grant's brother-in-law attempt to corner gold market; Crédit Mobilier scandal; "whiskey ring" and Native American trading post bribe taking; New York City and the Tweed Ring
      3. Foreign-policy successes of Johnson and Grant administrations: purchase of Alaska, favorable settlement of the *Alabama* claims
      4. 1872, Republicans disgusted by the scandals break with Grant and form Liberal Republican party
   B. The Liberals' Revolt
      1. Election of 1872: Liberal Republicans nominate Horace Greeley; Democrats endorse him also; Republicans renominate Grant
      2. Grant wins reelection, but split in Republican ranks seriously weakens Radical Reconstruction program in South
   C. The Panic of 1873
      1. Overspeculation leads to bank failures and financial panic
      2. Panic of 1873 touches off severe five-year depression: business failures, mass unemployment, heightened labor-management conflict, and disputes over nation's currency (greenbacks, silver, and "easy money" versus gold and "sound-money")

The Crises of Reconstruction, 1865–1877   **179**

3. Depression and problems spawned by it further lessen and divert Republican interest in Reconstruction

D. *Reconstruction and the Constitution*
   1. Supreme Court issues decisions that undermine Radical Reconstruction
   2. *Slaughterhouse* case, *U.S.* v. *Reese,* and *U.S.* v. *Cruikshank* weaken enforcement of Fourteenth and Fifteenth Amendments
   3. Supreme Court declares Civil Rights Act of 1875 and Ku Klux Klan Act (1871) unconstitutional

E. *Republicans in Retreat*
   1. By 1870s Republicans are abandoning their Reconstruction policy
   2. Reasons: Republicans more interested in economic growth than black rights; most Radical leaders dead; voters tired of "the southern question" and "the Negro question"

V. Reconstruction Abandoned

A. *"Redeeming" the South*
   1. After 1872 Congress pardons almost all former Confederates
   2. These former Confederates and South's rising class of businessmen lead Democratic party in drive to redeem South from Republican rule
   3. Democrats use economic pressure, intimidation, and violence to regain control of southern states
   4. Redemption (return of Democrats to power) results in tax cuts, elimination of public works and social services, enactment of laws favoring landlords over tenants and stripping freedmen of rights
   5. Some blacks migrate from South (exodus movement); most trapped where they are by debt and poverty

B. *The Election of 1876*
   1. Republicans nominate Rutherford B. Hayes; Democrats, Samuel J. Tilden
   2. Tilden wins popular vote, but because of fraud and intimidation at the polls, electoral count in four states disputed
   3. Special electoral commission, stacked in favor of Republicans, awards all disputed votes to Hayes
   4. Democrats refuse to accept findings until compromise worked out between southern Democrats and Republican supporters of Hayes
   5. Compromise of 1877: southerners accept Hayes as president; Republicans promise to let Democrats take over last Republican Reconstruction governments in Louisiana, South Carolina, and Florida; remove remaining troops from South; give federal patronage to southern Democrats; provide federal aid for railroads and other internal improvements in South
   6. Blacks abandoned to mercies of vindictive white southerners

Copyright © Houghton Mifflin Company. All rights reserved.

Vocabulary

The following terms are used in Chapter 16. To understand the chapter fully, it is important that you know what each of them means.

suffrage the vote; the right to vote

enfranchisement the giving of the rights of citizenship and voting (the taking away of these rights is called *disenfranchisement*)

allegiance faithfulness and obligation to a person, idea, country, or government

amnesty a general pardon for offenses against a government

status quo antebellum the way things were before the war

yeomen nonslaveholding, small landowning farmers

referendum the procedure of submitting legislative measures to voters for approval or rejection

mandate instruction about policy given or supposed to be given by the voters to a legislative body or government

confiscate to seize private property by government authority

impeachment the charging of a public official, such as a judge or president, with misconduct in office

vigilantes members of extralegal citizens' groups organized to maintain order and punish offenses

electorate the body of persons entitled to vote in an election

coalition a combination or alliance among different groups, parties, or states in support of a particular cause, individual, or purpose

writ of habeas corpus a formal order requiring that an arrested person be brought before a judge or court and either charged with a specific crime or released; the right to such a writ is guaranteed in the U.S. Constitution

autonomy self-government, independence

capital wealth (especially money) that can be used to produce more wealth

segregation the act of separating or setting apart from others, especially on the basis of race (the undoing of such separation is called *desegregation* or *integration*)

collateral security or property pledged for the payment of a loan

speculator one who trades in commodities, securities, or land in the hope of making a profit from changes in their market value; a person who engages in business transactions that involve considerable risk but offer the chance of large gains

Identifications

After reading Chapter 16, you should be able to identify and explain the historical significance of each of the following:

Lincoln's 10 percent plan, the Wade-Davis bill

Thirteenth Amendment

black codes

Freedmen's Bureau

Thaddeus Stevens and the Radical Republicans

Civil Rights Act of 1866

Fourteenth Amendment

Reconstruction Act of 1867

Tenure of Office Act

Fifteenth Amendment

Elizabeth Cady Stanton and Susan B. Anthony

carpetbaggers and scalawags

Enforcement Acts (Ku Klux Klan Act)

Civil Rights Cases, 1883

Jay Gould and Jim Fisk

Crédit Mobilier

William M. Tweed

Liberal Republicans and Horace Greeley

greenbacks and the Greenback party

redemption

"exodus" movement

Rutherford B. Hayes, Samuel J. Tilden, and the Compromise of 1877

Multiple-Choice Questions

Circle the letter of the item that best completes each statement or answers the question.

1. Lincoln's plan of reconstructing the South
   a. required southern states to enfranchise blacks.
   b. required that 50 percent or more of white voters in a former Confederate state take an oath of allegiance to the Union before a new state government could be established.
   c. was intended to gain the support of southern Unionists and attract them to a southern Republican party.
   d. was eventually accepted by Congress.

2. Which of the following statements about Andrew Johnson is *incorrect*?
   a. He wanted to exclude the planters from political leadership in the South, but then he undermined his intention by granting so many pardons to this group.
   b. He cared deeply about obtaining just treatment for the freedmen.
   c. He was a lifelong Democrat with no interest in building the strength of the Republican party.
   d. He vetoed all of the congressional Reconstruction acts, only to have Congress override his vetoes.

3. The black codes
   a. were imposed by Congress on former Confederate states.
   b. guaranteed blacks such basic liberties as freedom of movement and employment, the right to testify in court, and the use of all public facilities.
   c. were seen by Thaddeus Stevens and other Radical Republicans as a necessary legal step to help blacks make the transition from slavery to freedom.
   d. were laws passed by the Johnson governments in the South to keep blacks as a semifree, cheap labor force.

4. Which of their plans did Radical Republicans persuade Congress to embody in the Reconstruction acts and the Fourteenth and Fifteenth Amendments?
   a. black suffrage, a period of military occupation of the South, temporary exclusion of former Confederates from voting and officeholding
   b. confiscation and redistribution of land in the South, imprisonment of former Confederate leaders
   c. forty acres and a mule for each freedman, temporary disenfranchisement of whites, enfranchisement of blacks
   d. exile of Jefferson Davis and other former Confederate leaders, upholding of all Civil War debts, extending right to vote to all citizens older than age twenty-one

5. Andrew Johnson was impeached but not convicted because
   a. he proved that he had not violated the Tenure of Office Act.
   b. he resigned before the Senate voted on his guilt.
   c. seven Republicans, fearing that the president's removal would upset the balance of power among the three branches of government, voted "not guilty" with the Democrats.
   d. the Supreme Court ruled that he had not engaged in misconduct in office.

6. The Fifteenth Amendment
   a. defines citizenship and requires states to extend to all persons equal protection of the laws.
   b. states that no one shall be denied the right to vote because of race, color, or previous condition of servitude.
   c. extends suffrage to all citizens age twenty-one or older.
   d. gives Congress the power to deny seats in the House to states that do not allow black men to vote.

7. In the Republican Reconstruction governments of the South, the group that held most political offices consisted of
   a. carpetbaggers.
   b. scalawags.
   c. blacks.
   d. the planter elite.

8. The Republican Reconstruction governments of the South
   a. gave the region the most honest, efficient governments it had ever had.
   b. excluded almost all whites from officeholding and were run almost exclusively by blacks.
   c. created public-school systems, built and repaired roads and bridges, and opened institutions to care for orphans and the disabled.
   d. cut taxes and passed laws favoring the interests of landlords over those of tenants and sharecroppers.

9. The sharecropping and crop-lien systems that developed in the post–Civil War South
   a. contributed to soil depletion, agricultural backwardness, and southern poverty.
   b. reduced the portion of southern land owned and controlled by the planter elite.
   c. forced most black people out of agriculture and into southern cities.
   d. tied white planters and black tenants together economically but had no effect on white small farmers.

10. The Compromise of 1877
    a. allowed the peaceful inauguration of a Democratic president in exchange for promises that the Democrats would enforce the Fourteenth and Fifteenth Amendments.
    b. allowed the peaceful inauguration of a Republican president in exchange for federal removal of all troops from the South and promises of federal aid for internal improvements in the South.
    c. marked the final acceptance by the white South of full equality for blacks in exchange for federal aid in rebuilding the war-damaged South.
    d. allowed the peaceful inauguration of Rutherford B. Hayes in exchange for recognition of and federal help in paying off the Confederate war debt.

11. Most historians today view Radical Reconstruction as a democratic experiment that failed because it
    a. left blacks without property and thus economically unable to defend their political rights.
    b. relied on excessive military force instead of political persuasion.
    c. was unrealistic in its expectation that illiterate blacks could be turned into responsible citizens overnight.
    d. was overly vindictive and harsh toward all white southerners.

12. *Grantism* is associated with
    a. efficient but harsh enforcement of the Radical Reconstruction program in the South.
    b. the first attempts by the federal government to provide adequately for the needs of Native Americans.
    c. the favoring of the needs of labor and the poor over the demands of railroad and manufacturing interests.
    d. political corruption, bribe taking, and dishonest get-rich-quick schemes.

Essay Questions

1. Compare and contrast Lincoln's, Johnson's, and Congress's plans of reconstruction (as represented by the Reconstruction acts of 1867–1868 and the Fourteenth and Fifteenth Amendments). What were the objectives of each plan? Why did each fail to achieve its goals?

2. Discuss the transformation of southern agriculture during the Reconstruction period. Why did the sharecropping and crop-lien systems evolve? What were the consequences of those systems for the economy of the South and for white and black farmers?

3. Discuss the achievements and failures of the Republican Reconstruction governments in the South. Who supported and who opposed them? Why? Why and how were they driven from power?

4. Imagine that you are a Freedmen's Bureau agent in the South during the Reconstruction period. Using the information in Chapter 16, write an account of what you have seen black people doing and experiencing. As such an agent, how have you been involved with the blacks in your district?

5. Write an essay discussing the Grant administration. What were its policies on Reconstruction and the freedmen? What was meant by *Grantism* and Grant's "Great Barbecue"? What successes and failures did the administration have in foreign policy? Why did the Liberal Republicans break with Grant?

Answers to Multiple-Choice Questions

1a. No. His plan made no mention of giving black men the vote.
1b. No. He required only 10 percent take the oath.
1c. Yes. See page 311.
1d. No. It never was.

2a. No. The statement is correct.
2b. Yes. This statement is *incorrect*. Johnson's statements and actions, such as vetoing the continuation of the Freedman's Bureau and opposing the 14th Amendment, showed that protecting the freedmen was not high on his agenda. See pages 313, 314-315.
2c. No. See 2a.
2d. No. See 2a.

3a. No. They were passed by the southern state governments established under Johnson's plan of reconstruction.
3b. No. They denied blacks freedom of movement and employment, forcing them to sign long-term labor contracts that kept them on plantations. They were not allowed to testify in court against whites, and all public facilities were segregated.
3c. No. The Radical and Moderate Republicans saw these codes for what they were: a southern attempt to strictly limit the freedom of the former slaves and keep them as a source of cheap agricultural labor for the South.
3d. Yes. See pages 312-313.

4a. Yes. See pages 314-317.
4b. No. Congress never agreed to either of these things. The failure to redistribute land to the freedmen was probably the greatest weakness of the Radical Reconstruction program.
4c. No. Again the failure to provide land for blacks left them impoverished and unable to exercise their political rights.
4d. No. Congress did none of these.

5a. No. He probably did not prove this.
5b. No. Johnson did not resign.
5c. Yes. See pages 315-316.
5d. No. The Supreme Court was not involved.

6a. No. That is in the 14th Amendment.
6b. Yes. See page 316.
6c. No. It did not give women the right to vote.
6d. No. That is in the 14th Amendment.

7a. No. They held the second most.
7b. Yes. See page 318.
7c. No. Though they were the biggest and most loyal supporters of these governments, they held fewer positions.
7d. No. Most of them were barred from office holding during Radical Reconstruction.

8a. No. Most of them were tainted by corruption.
8b. No. White carpetbaggers and scalawags held most of the offices and mostly ran them.
8c. Yes. See page 318.
8d. No. The Democratic governments that replaced the Republican Reconstruction governments did that.

9a. Yes. See page 324.
9b. No. The planter elite hung on to the land they had owned before the Civil War.
9c. No. About 75 percent of blacks in the cotton growing states were sharecroppers and tenants.
9d. No. More sharecroppers were white than black.

10a. No. Tilden, the Democrat, went down to defeat.
10b. Yes. See page 330.
10c. No. The white South had no intention of accepting full equality for blacks; even most of the Republicans no longer believed in that goal.
10d. No. Hayes did become president, but paying off the Confederate debt was not part of the bargain.

11a. Yes. See page 331.
11b. No. Just the opposite. The Federal government never put enough military force behind it.
11c. No. In fact, blacks participated quite successfully in politics until white terror tactics deprived them of their political rights.
11d. No. All of the reconstruction plans were quite mild toward white southerners, even those who had held high office in the Confederate government.

12a. No. Grant's enforcement of Radical Reconstruction was neither efficient nor harsh.
12b. No. Not what the term refers to.
12c. No. Not what characterized the Grant administration.
12d. Yes. See page 325.